IRISH POETRY AFTER YEATS

Seven Poets

By MAURICE HARMON

Fenians and Fenianism

J. M. Synge Centenary Papers

The Poetry of Thomas Kinsella: "With Darkness for a Nest"

Select Bibliography for the Study of Anglo-Irish Literature and Its Backgrounds: An Irish Studies Handbook

Richard Murphy: Poet of Two Traditions

Image and Illusion: Anglo-Irish Literature and Its Contexts

IRISH POETRY
AFTER YEATS

Austin Clarke
Patrick Kavanagh
Denis Devlin
Richard Murphy   *Seven Poets*
Thomas Kinsella
John Montague
Seamus Heaney

Edited by

MAURICE HARMON

LITTLE, BROWN AND COMPANY

BOSTON   TORONTO

LIBRARY OF CONGRESS CATALOG CARD NO.
81-82577
FIRST AMERICAN EDITION

ACKNOWLEDGEMENTS

Poems by Austin Clarke are from *Pilgrimage, Night and Morning, Ancient Lights,
Too Great a Vine, Flight to Africa, Mnemosyne Lay in Dust, A Sermon on
Swift:* by kind permission of Mrs. Nora Clarke, and The Dolmen Press. Poems by
Patrick Kavanagh are from *Ploughman, The Great Hunger, A Soul for Sale,
Come Dance with Kitty Stobling, Collected Poems:* by kind permission of
Mrs. Catherine Kavanagh. Poems by Denis Devlin are from *Collected Poems,*
The Dolmen Press. Poems by Richard Murphy are from *High Island* ("Sailing to an
Island," "The Woman of the House," "The Last Galway Hooker," "The Battle
of Aughrim," "Walking on Sunday," "Pat Cloherty's Version of *The Maisie*,"
"Coppersmith," "Nocturne," "Stormpelrel," copyright © 1974 by Richard Murphy,
"Seals at High Island" copyright © 1973 by Richard Murphy,
"The Reading Lesson" copyright © 1971 by Richard Murphy), reprinted
by permission of Harper & Row, Publishers, Inc., and new poems by kind permission
of the poet. Poems by Thomas Kinsella are from *Another September,
Downstream, Nightwalker, New Poems, One, A Technical Supplement, Song of
the Night:* by kind permission of Mr. Kinsella, and The Dolmen Press.
Poems by John Montague are from *Poisoned Lands, A Chosen Light, Tides,
The Rough Field, A Slow Dance, The Great Cloak:* by kind permission of
Mr. Montague, and The Dolmen Press. Poems by Seamus Heaney are from *Death of
a Naturalist* ("Digging," "Follower," "At a Potato Digging,"
"Personal Helicon" copyright © 1966 by Seamus Heaney), *Door into the Dark*
("Thatcher," "The Wife's Tale," "Bogland" copyright © 1969 by Seamus Heaney),
Wintering Out ("Gifts of Rain," "The Tollund Man," "Summer Home"
copyright © 1972 by Seamus Heaney), *North* ("Viking Dublin: Trial Pieces,"
"Kinship," "A Constable Calls," "Exposure" copyright © 1975 by
Seamus Heaney), *Field Work* ("Casualty," "A Postcard from North Antrim,"
"Glanmore Sonnets," "The Otter," "Song" copyright © 1976, 1979
by Seamus Heaney), and new poems by kind permission of the poet.

PHOTO CREDITS

Austin Clarke: page 31, Jack McManus, *The Irish Times*. Patrick Kavanagh: page 68,
The Irish Times. Denis Devlin: page 88, *The Irish Times*. Richard Murphy: page 112,
Thomas Victor. Thomas Kinsella: page 136, Wolfhound Press. John Montague:
page 170, Willie Kelly. Seamus Heaney: page 196, Nancy Crampton.

CONTENTS

INTRODUCTION

There was one great advantage for the Irish writer who began his literary career after the Literary Revival had reached its peak: he could then aspire to a tradition that had been widely recognised and accepted. By the mid-twenties the idea of a separate and distinctive Irish tradition in English literature could not be denied. With the work of Synge, Yeats, Joyce and O'Casey, that tradition had established itself in the major genres and some of its characteristics were being noted: the gift for language, the mythological accretions, the rejection of naturalistic modes, the preference for the instinctive and the mystical, and the ability to alter the traditional iambic line with the rhythms and idiom of Anglo-Irish speech.

Such distinctions did not necessarily make the work of the next generations easier. They did establish standards by which younger writers could measure themselves and they did make it necessary for them to find a personal idiom and a distinctive voice. For a young poet in 1920 or 1930, the question was how not to write like Yeats and how to find areas not already dominated, or exhausted, by him. For the young poet in the fifties and sixties that question was less pressing. By then the whole issue of one's Irishness had become somewhat academic. Nevertheless, as Thomas Kinsella has argued, the potential Irish poet, looking back for available models, was in a position quite different from his British counterpart whose ancestry stretched back through the 19th century and the Romantics, Dryden, Milton, Shakespeare. For the Irish poet there was Yeats and behind him the weak poets of the 19th century and behind them a cultural shift to a different language and a virtually lost set of poetic values. Nevertheless the Yeatsian presence exerts a continuing influence. Thomas Kinsella's poems in *Another September* (1958), his first collection, show traces of that influence in their language and rhythms. Seamus Heaney's first collection, *Death of a Naturalist* (1966), is consciously different in its use of concrete, sensuous imagery from the vague and imprecise imagery of the early Yeats and his recent elegy, 'Casualty', about an eel-fisherman, uses the rhythms of Yeats's 'The Fisherman'.

Modern Irish poetry however cannot be properly understood apart from literary developments in England and America. Just as W. B. Yeats's career is traced against the background of London as well as Dublin, so the work of his successors may be seen within the perspectives of the changing conditions and directions of poetry in England and America. Yeats's legacy is a primary factor in the development of all Irish poets, but those who came after him were also affected by the modernist movement, by the various reactions against it, and by later developments. There are signs of indebtedness in all these poets to specific contemporary figures, such as Thomas Kinsella's to W. H. Auden, Seamus Heaney's to Robert Frost, or John Montague's to Gary Snyder. The fact of these relationships, and the list could be much extended, may be regarded as a sign of the openness of the poets to outside influences and of their determination to keep in touch with literary and intellectual developments elsewhere. Yeats's legacy, extensive and varied, is to be considered here under four aspects: his sense of the Irish past, its history, folklore, myth and legend; the symbol-making impulse of his imagination; the emphasis on personality; his belief in personal utterance.

Irish history, myth and legend fed his imagination from the start of his career. His imaginative concern for the Irish past, sometimes paralleled by or fused with a concern for events, places, people and ideas outside of Ireland, is an ingredient of his work from *The Wanderings of Oisin* (1889) to *Last Poems* (1939). From the beginning, he used myth, legend and history as a means of personal expression, not simply as objective narratives or themes. In this he was consciously different from his predecessor, Samuel Ferguson, who had written a number of poems based on Irish myth. It took Austin Clarke some time, in a period close to the Literary Revival, to grasp the significance of Yeats's personal handling of myth, and Clarke himself moves from general retellings in his early narratives to identification − with the Suibhne legend − and then to his intensely personal handling of the medieval scene. Since that time some poets have followed the example of Clarke and Yeats. There are, for example, John Montague's sense of a mythic hinterland to his Ulster background, Thomas Kinsella's psychic myth and Seamus Heaney's Jungian view of the past. But there are also Patrick Kavanagh's refusal to use the mythic method and Richard Murphy's determination to demythologise the past and the present. Yeats's sense of history or of heritage remains deep in all these poets. Their response to the past, their ways of handling it, and their selection of particular periods or figures within it vary from his and from each other, but the force of the past is undiminished. The evidence is that Patrick Kavanagh's rejection of Culture for cultural continuity was replaced in John Montague's generation and in Seamus Heaney's by a capacity to invoke and absorb as much of both as was available and useful.

Yeats rooted his work in his own country. Ireland and the matter of Ireland were the objects of his immediate concern, but his approach was shaped by his attraction to the symbolist movement. Initially he drew his symbols from Ireland − Cuchulain, Fergus, the hosting of the sidhe, the black pig, Hanrahan – but later, as his vision expanded, he called upon familiar and traditional symbols – Leda, Byzantium, the Second Coming. Whatever the source, his symbolic system of bird and beast, sun, moon and gyre, is largely responsible for the enormous force of his poetry. Traditional symbols, having been used recurrently in many different contexts, call up a dense variety of meanings, emotions, and associations. By writing *A Vision* he gave his ideas, memories, images and symbols place and interrelation within a comprehensive system. That system enriches the poetry, making it elaborate and rich in implication. Later poets would not always want to achieve a similar density and complexity, but the value of multiple, mutually-enriching associations within an individual body of work remained. None of the younger poets, after Clarke and Denis Devlin, actively tried to construct a system on the same scale as Yeats's. Kinsella's approach, which is closest, owes as much to Pound as to Yeats. Kavanagh deliberately cut down the range of reference and symbols to the area of a small farm, although this anti-mythic stance, since it was so restrictive did not always appeal to later poets. In their case the recurrence of image and theme is the natural result of the imagination's tendency to use a defining pattern of images, a sign more of artistic integrity than of a conscious system. Denis Devlin did not evolve a system, but he has much of Yeats's symbol-making approach. In his work also the imagination transforms what is actual and objective.

Yeats believed in the transforming and recreative power of the imagination, but he wanted his poems to convey the impression of being spoken by a man within the ordinary circumstances of his life. At the same time, he liked to put on masks, to dramatise, to speak with authority and with power. Thinking in antitheses, he carried on a public debate with himself in which he considered the opposing claims of nature and art, body and soul, youth and age, passion and wisdom. The fact is that his poems give the impression of talk even though they are quite unlike actual speech, especially in diction and syntax. We hear them as natural and spontaneous and find their form congenial, tending not to notice how digressive they sometimes are, or how unexpected in their intensities or modulations of feeling. Yeats both creates an imperious persona and achieves the effect of personal utterance. In full flight he has a powerful and hypnotic voice, excited, passionate, stylized, sweeping or extravagant. The manner went out of fashion quickly enough. We find it in Denis Devlin, but not in Austin Clarke or Patrick Kavanagh. The latter's assumption of the role of the poet as fool is a cunning deflation of the Yeatsian personality. Austin Clarke's use of an almost invisible self is in large measure a retreat from Yeats's imperious presence and to some degree a response to T. S. Eliot's insistence on the extinction of the personality of the author. The cult of personality was resisted, but the preference for personal utterance lingered on. Irish poetry on the whole is written for the ear rather than the eye. We hear the poetry of Patrick Kavanagh, Austin Clarke and Denis Devlin. There is a characteristic voice in each case. We hear too the distinguishing voices of their successors, even when the appearance of the poem on the page, or the use of space, indicates that they have also learnt their trade from poets outside of the Irish oral tradition. But then, too, Eliot's stress on the auditory imagination, so strongly favoured by Heaney, means that the modern poet tends to be sensitive to the texture of the poem, to its evocation in sound and rhythm of things hidden in the depths of the subconscious. Kinsella's *Notes from the Land of the Dead* (1973) is just one striking example of this poetic mode. So if there is in Irish poetry a special response to the speaking voice, that voice may be, in Eliot's terminology, of the first kind.

Yeats also contributed significantly to the development of modern poetry. His sense of organic unity, for example, prepared the way for the modernist juxtaposition of dissimilar elements within a poem. Until the publication of *The Waste Land* (1922) the prevailing poetic mode was a kind of honest accuracy and control, such as we find in *The Wild Swans at Coole* (1919). The poem is reflective and leisurely in movement; the diction is not much removed from colloquial speech; the subject is actual, everyday experience; the form is traditional. But the form of *The Waste Land* is not traditional; its structure is alogical, placing separate and often disparate units of meaning side by side. We read it as a complex of elements and think of all its parts, its non-temporal set of interrelated images, as being present at the same time. Ezra Pound's *Cantos* and William Carlos Williams's *Paterson* in their open, non-sequential structures, together with *The Waste Land* had an important effect on modern poetry.

These and the critical theories of Ezra Pound, T. S. Eliot and others trained poets to construct formally complex and compressed ways of writing. But William Carlos Williams, whose work became influential in Ireland and England after the second World War, wrote in a plain, unpretentious manner; his poems are fresh; they find delight in things perceived and have an unhindered momentum that is quite different from the dense, compacted work of T. S. Eliot and Ezra Pound. Poets generally reacted against their kind of poetry, against the large subject, against the ambitious emotional gesture. Clarity, rational control and the avoidance of obscurity returned to favour. The divisions which may be drawn in English and American poetry from the establishment of

the modernist mode in the 1920's to the arrival of a neo-modernist
conservatism in the 1950's is paralleled in Ireland by the differences
between the Clarke-Kavanagh-Devlin generation and that of the
Kinsella-Montague-Murphy generation. Not that the later poets ignored
Pound's advice to make it new, or had not learnt from Eliot's precise
sense of the possibilities of tone or phrasing, or his concept of the
inseparability of past and present. But they learnt too from Carlos
Williams and from his many successors, they studied his control of line,
and his variation of line-length according to the sequence of thought
and feeling.

Yet, no matter how we may link Irish poets with technical or
thematic developments and trends elsewhere, the fact is that they
tend to be independent of movements and not to be radical innovators.
They do not think of themselves as a school or movement, however we
may detect similarities of sensibility, or of approach, or of emphasis in
their work at a particular period. The fact that the literature is usually
affected by the specific Irish influences inevitably sets them apart from
their contemporaries. Clarke's absorption of Gaelic forms and prosody,
for example, his immersion in native traditions, or his later reliance on
localised event — inevitably makes the textures and rhythms of his
work, its allusions and cultural resonances different from what we find
in Eliot or Pound, in Carlos Williams or Wallace Stevens. His example is
a powerful stimulus to any Irish poet who wants to deepen the
imaginative links and reverberations between the individual self and the
Irish background, both present and past. It can, for example, also be
claimed that Irish poets since the Fifties have shared the sense of
depression that is present in both English and American poets; that in
their work too the speaking self acts in isolation; that the thrust of their
work is toward whatever insights or consolations the individual may
gain; that it is confessional. These observations are true of Montague
and Kinsella, but they are not true of Seamus Heaney, whose explorations of the past have a more positive and self-delighting quality. The
auditory imagination, in his case, is not just a matter of sounding the
history of the countryside in its place-names and pronunciations, it
uses words as symptoms of human history, memory and attachments.

The directions taken by Irish poetry after Yeats may be studied in
the work of the seven poets included in this anthology. They could
also be seen in the work of other poets, such as John Hewitt, Louis
MacNeice, Brian Coffey and Padraic Fallon. John Hewitt's attempts to
define his relationships with his ancestors, with the divisions of
Northern Ireland, and with the rest of Ireland make his work very
central to Irish literature. Hewitt as chronicler and recorder of social

and cultural history resembles Clarke, the memorialist. His acceptance of a province reminds us of Kavanagh's trust in his parish. His 'grammar' of a 'dialect' anticipates Heaney's attention to the possibilities of the auditory imagination. Louis MacNeice illustrates the dilemma of the Anglo-Irish writer. In this he resembles Richard Murphy, but even more so in their common allegiance to the west of Ireland. MacNeice's urban world and involvement with international politics reminds us how close Irish literary life often is to England and elsewhere. His urban sensibility and sceptical intelligence finds echoes in later poets, but especially in Derek Mahon. Mahon's origins are urban; his concern is how to write from a context which, as he sees it, has no mythology or symbolism built into it, Belfast in this respect being different from Dublin. He writes poetry of place and of people which are definitions of a personal background and he uses a modernist idiom and a shielding irony of manner. Filtering images from Beckett and other artists to provide an oblique illumination of his own background, his poem's touch fleetingly on his childhood contexts which are a founding element in his work. There is also the tendency for the subliminal to surface through the concrete images and personal references and he is often close to Heaney in the sense of the deposits of the past affecting the present. Mahon is conscious of MacNeice as a forerunner, just as he is conscious of Heaney as immediate direction-finder. MacNeice's abstract, philosophical mind, however, somewhat rare in Irish poetry, together with his dialectical concept of life brings him closer to Yeats than to anyone else. In his philosophical and metaphysical manner he is also close to Brian Coffey whose subject matter is human nature which he considers apart from its local and immediate temporal contexts. Coffey's modernistic mode of disjointed images and phrases makes his work much different in style and tone from Yeats and from most other Irish poets, with the exception of Devlin and some much younger figures. Nevertheless, his major poem, *Advent* (1975) with its sense of expectancy and of potentiality is much closer to Kinsella and Heaney than one might expect. The fact of the fundamental Catholicism of his thought joins him with Austin Clarke and Padraic Fallon. Fallon's *Poems* (1974) celebrate life in the west of Ireland. He delights in the resonances of words. His imagination, like Yeats's, transforms reality or recreates it in larger terms and his work has a fine openness to experience. At times it is directed inward to the subliminal and dark places of the self, and at times backward into myth.

A more inclusive and comprehensive anthology would have ranged more widely among the poets contemporary with Clarke and with

Kinsella and could have included work by poets born since 1939. Their absence is not to be taken as a reflection on the quality of their work or on its importance. The developments in Irish poetry since Heaney and its relationships with his work and with that of his immediate predecessors need separate illustration and may be detected in other anthologies listed below. But the purpose of this anthology is to offer a meaningful representation of each poet's work so that it can be studied effectively, and read with a sense of the poet's overall achievements. It was essential therefore that only a limited number of poets should be included, and the seven poets selected between them reflect major aspects of Irish poetry after Yeats. In the first generation Patrick Kavanagh and Austin Clarke express one kind of reaction by being stubbornly Irish, the one immersing himself in the matter of Ireland, the other curtailing himself mainly to his rural background, and both reacting against the Yeats' manner or certain aspects of it. Denis Devlin, to escape such restrictions, launched himself into the wider stream of European culture and availed of techniques which were present in continental poetry. The next three poets belong to the renewal of the Fifties and Sixties. Consciously cosmopolitan as young poets, they have maintained a balance between their awareness of what was happening outside of Ireland and their certainty that they can find imaginative nourishment in the contexts of their own immediate past and that of their country. In John Montague's work we find increasingly the deprivations of Northern Ireland. Behind his work lies not only Kavanagh's reliance on the parish, but the exploration of racial and cultural divisions that permeates the work of John Hewitt, and Louis MacNeice. Richard Murphy provides clear evidence also of cultural division. Born into an Ascendancy background, his work plays against that of Yeats in a manner quite different from Padraic Fallon's, which combines some of the main features of Clarke and Kavanagh and has a particular fascination with the work of Yeats. Thomas Kinsella shows how fruitful Dublin has become in the literature. His attachment to particular places in the city, to particular members of his own family, to a sense of the dark backward and abysm of time carries forward the identification of Clarke and Joyce with the city. His explorations of background lead into a kind of myth of artistic or creative energy, within the artist himself, within his forebears, within the race and within the natural order. Finally, Seamus Heaney's rooting of his work in a rural background resembles Kavanagh's in the sense of continuities, but goes deeper into the visible and auditory potentialities of a particular region which he expands to include its parallels in Europe. All benefit from the example of Yeats and from modern poetry in general.

Yeats's influence on Austin Clarke was inescapable. He wrote first in imitation of the early Yeats by writing epic narratives based mainly on the Celtic past. It was not until 1929 that *Pilgrimage* presented an entirely different world of monk and scholar, sinner and saint in pre-Norman Ireland. It defines his sense of himself as a new voice in Irish poetry: objective, formal and classical where the poetry of the Revival had been subjective and romantic, exploring the Celtic-Romanesque world instead of the Old Irish period that Yeats had sponsored, and drawing specifically on forms and conventions found in Old Irish and in modern Gaelic poetry. In this volume Clarke begins to face up to what he calls the 'drama of racial conscience', a subject ignored by poets of the Revival. He begins also to react to the restrictions of Church and State in post-revolutionary Ireland and this carries forward to the compressed and satirical 'Celebrations', and from the compact 'Penal Laws' to the looser 'The Envy of Poor Lovers'. In time he develops the artistic possibilities of the Celtic-Romanesque world, but 'Pilgrimage' itself with its reverent tone, its formal decorum, and its celebration of artistic and spiritual achievements is his most unqualified tribute.

Night and Morning (1938) expresses the Irish Catholic conscience in a painfully personal manner. Clarke's method of placing the desire for intellectual and sexual freedom within a context of religious and social restraint is particularly attuned to the tightly inwrought style of such poems as 'Night and Morning' and 'Tenebrae'. In one he speaks of a soul tormented by the conflict between intellectual freedom and emotional need. In the other he dramatises the state of a man attracted by what he partially rejects.

Clarke's next collection of poems *Ancient Lights, Poems and Satires,* appeared in 1955. With this and in particular with the collected *Later Poems* (1961) he astonished his younger contemporaries by being so vigorous, so flexible, and so honest about himself. For the next twenty years, while they progressed into middle age, he matched their development with a succession of volumes of remarkable and growing power, in which there were poems of indisputable merit, such as 'Martha Blake at Fifty-One', 'Japanese Print', 'Burial of an Irish President', and a number of autobiographical poems of which *Mnemosyne Lay in Dust* (1966) is the most remarkable. He was, during the last twenty years of his life, at once the resident satirist and the memorialist, marking public and private events with wry humour or occasional outrage, and moving with steady courage from the dense allusive manner and the wrenched syntax of 'The Loss of Strength' to the more fluent style of 'Burial of an Irish President', from the elaborate internal structure and multiple verbal meanings of 'Celebrations' to the fluid simplicity of 'Usufruct', a quietly humorous definition of self and circumstances. He could be satiric or tender, testy or erotic at will; and the particularity and precision of 'Pilgrimage' and the intimate sense of the Irish landscape stayed with him through each volume.

Clarke affirms the importance of the natural world in 'Ancient Lights' in which he moves from the fears produced by church teachings into the absolution of the rain. In 'The Loss of Strength' he fuses the curtailments of age with national diminishments, but relies on the consolations of nature: 'Lesser bits of life console us: / Nature at jest in light and shade'. In 'Cypress Grove' he laments a lost elegance, but animates the landscape with things seen and heard and felt.

Throughout his work, the humane voice is dominant in 'Penal Law' and 'The Envy of Poor Lovers' no less than in 'Tenebrae', in the recreations of the Celtic-Romanesque world of 'Pilgrimage', in all the compassionate poems of the later period and in the studied detachment of that most tender of them all 'Martha Blake at Fifty-One'. This poem also is about the conflict of soul and body and contrasts the romance of the spiritual with the realities of physical distress.

Austin Clarke has been resolutely himself, so that if it comes to arguing about the Irishness of an Irish poet, or the international relevance of an Irish poet, or whether a particular poet is or is not within the Irish tradition, Clarke's achievement, based so decisively on an acceptance of himself and his situation and grounded so thoroughly, though not exclusively, on the varied strands of the Irish heritage, affects our view of the whole complex issue.

Patrick Kavanagh by contrast spurned antiquity; he took his material instinctively from what he knew best, the life of a small farm in Co. Monaghan. It was the first intimate and authoritative response to rural life in poetry. Behind Kavanagh is not so much the work of Padraic Colum or F. R. Higgins as the Gaelic poets of the 18th century. His is a lyrical voice, responsive to the magic of nature: he would commemorate, not the riches of a cultural heritage, but the ways of people and places, the habits of daily life, the natural rhythms of speech; and this is another kind of acceptance, of the ordinary, the parochial, the limited mind, the Catholic conscience on the one hand and beside it, sometimes in union, but often in disharmony, with it — the plenitude of the earth and its seasonal flowering, its great natural processes. The tragedy comes when someone like Maguire in 'The Great Hunger', resembling Martha Blake, takes what his mother and his Church say so literally that he stifles the operation of nature in himself. Maguire rushes beyond the ordinary for an Absolute, missing what is within the reach of his senses. So Kavanagh, detached from what he describes, records with love and authority the tragedy of missed opportunities, making Maguire unable to see how the light of imagination may grow from the clay.

Kavanagh's vision is based on a sense of joy in life, of delight in the natural world. His openness to this lies at the heart of his work. Within his lyrical delight in light and water, field and furrow, flower and weed, is a note of mariolatry: his childhood training in Catholic practices infuses his adult poetry in an unselfconscious way. He delights in the magical moment, the rapt wonder which is presented as a romantic prolongation, a moment of union with the mysterious, a moment of communion. At his best his poetry becomes a note of love, even of physical, imaginative union with the feminine earth. But within the tone of love is also a note of loss, of separation through time and experience, from the childhood wonder. His work is an instructive account of that process of being uprooted that is so central to the experience of the Irish writer for whom, it seems, the process of becoming a writer, with its inevitable degree of analysis and definition, with its opening towards other worlds, of the city and of the outside world, involves a detachment from the familiar: the penalties of self-discovery may be the end of innocence and the beginning of alienation. Kavanagh faces this issue in his later poetry of recovery; his life in Dublin often produced poetry of anger, as well as poetry of loss, but it finally gave way to a happy carelessness, an indifference to issues and causes, and an imaginative repossession of the earth.

His rural world added to Irish poetry: what he drew into poetry, what he redeemed from loss, what he earned out of his personal separation from his childhood world, stands as a model for other poets with a rural background, such as Montague and Heaney. In turn they too would commemorate the values and customs of a rural world, they too would respond, as he did, to the destructive, indifferent advance of progress. Yeats could foresee the implacable forces let loose by a second coming, could enlarge that concept to a cosmic scope. His successors see it less largely. Kinsella's concept of evil encroachment or evil let loose by human wills is in its abstract formulation akin to Yeats's in metaphorical force, but he also sees its operation in particular instances; at the same time his examples of positive force are rooted in particular individuals and in the artistic act. Austin Clarke's response to destruction accumulates in his later poetry in references to the despoliation of the countryside, the ravishment of Dublin, the social and religious oppression, and the consequent diminished opportunities for the imagination.

For Kavanagh, Monaghan was more important than Munich and indeed for Austin Clarke, despite some later observations on Ireland's relationship with Europe or Africa and on America, the world of Ireland was enough. Denis Devlin, on the other hand, was cosmopolitan, partly because his career as a diplomat took him out of Ireland but mainly because his instinct was to get out, to follow Joyce and Beckett, to enrich the native by grafting it onto the European. He attempted to overcome the parochial by building into his poetry a system of cosmopolitan reference, largely French, so that he owes more to Aragon, Eluard and St. John Perse than to Yeats.

'Memoirs of a Turcoman Diplomat' is one of a number of poems in which his diplomatic profession provides the tone and the texture. In his poetry language is sometimes a safeguard against that which is alien, sometimes an embodiment of that which is appealing. The condition of exile, involving absence from home or country, love or religion, also involves exposure to other cultures, other settings, other ideologies. It is appropriate that his poetry should be reflective, capable of a wide range of feeling, and that its rhythms should be responsive to the subtle movements of the spirit. The treatment in 'Memoirs of a Turcoman Diplomat' of the oppositions between history and religion, on the one hand and individual response to beauty, love and art on the other introduces a set of concerns that are present throughout Devlin's poetry. Nor is this poem as remote as its settings and allusions might suggest, since the analogies between Turkey and Ireland are many and fruitful.

His career as a poet draws attention to a recurrent attitude among Irish writers, although not limited to them. Based on the feeling that life in Ireland is restrictive and provincial, they seek wider literary and imaginative horizons. Austin Clarke's turning to former periods is similar to this; he found not only congenial regions for his imagination, but could use the past in a variety of ways, revitalising it and his own poetry, could open it up for contemporary use, as a frame of reference for critical comment on his own period. Devlin's mind turned outward to embrace the larger European cultural dimensions. Such an attitude is not inherently more valid or more justified than Clarke's preference for pre-Norman Ireland or Kavanagh's love of the parish. It may be argued that Kavanagh's poetry travels better, since it contains so much of the world of nature and of human nature. It may be argued that Clarke loads himself with too many historical and topical chains, so that his range of vision, even when dealing with contemporary life, is often demandingly local. It may equally be argued that Devlin's communication of the European and the Irish, or of the Christian and the Irish Catholic, is too densely centrifugal. But the only argument is that of effectiveness. Of these three no one choice is inherently the more valid.

In Devlin we frequently find the anguished or tormented persona, an 'I' figure, intensely involved with and the victim of experience, usually of love or of religion. The intensity is conveyed through the language which is sometimes surrealistic and at all times elegant, even dandyistic, and concerned with the manner of its saying. In love with language, using it like a virtuoso, his inner stress of feeling puts strain on the syntax; as in 'Farewell and Good', where the harsh, blunt language conveys the drama of the individual situation.

'The Colours of Love' also reveals Devlin's delight in language. One of its interesting aspects, significant as an example of his attempt to marry the local and the remote, is the way in which the landscape and social reality of the west of Ireland is transformed within the poem. The actual is given little autonomy. Where Synge or O'Flaherty respected what they recorded from the outside, Devlin subordinates it to his own creative purposes. The descriptive details shift into emblem and allegory.

That process of absorption and transformation may also be observed in 'Jansenist Journey' where the personal and familial become part of a pilgrim's progress in which the actual is made emblematical. When the process is not achieved, the result is an uncertainty of grasp, as in 'Lough Derg', which is a meditation on the nature of the Irish way of penitence and of Christianity. The poem joins the Irish and the European in a many-sided and compact manner.

That Devlin is a poet of great power is apparent in 'The Passion of Christ', a sequence of vivid, epigrammatic poems, each of which is a gloss on the Biblical account. Devlin's intellectual passion may be seen in the compressed and paradoxical poems which challenge the sense and the intelligence, defining and asserting significant, homilectic interpretations. The whole sequence, which is rich in memorable lines and phrases, and dramatic in its vividness of image and definition, is an exploration of Christ's passion and triumph over death to discover and declare their meaning. Throughout is the feeling of moving with conviction towards its final celebration of Christ's ascension and transfiguration, an accomplishment similar to Devlin's own need for a poetry that transforms feeling and events by an act of linguistic transfiguration. The serenity of tone in the poem's conclusion reveals a radiance and confidence found nowhere else in his work. In Christ's ascension the world of doubt and darkness is not only overcome but given a place in the scheme of things.

For Richard Murphy the problem was to reconcile the traditions of the Protestant Ascendancy and the Catholic peasantry. 'What I really wanted to get clear were my origins and where we came from and who we were and what our past was.' Although that observation was made about his long poem 'The Battle of Aughrim', it is central to his work. 'Sailing to an Island', partly the record of an actual voyage and partly an archetypal journey of initiation and self-discovery is a proving of the self, a passing beyond the walled grounds of the Big House to the freer, more imaginative and more natural life of the native Irish. Many of his poems have this quality of a test of the spirit; their attention is directed to the skill with which something is achieved, an action, or a way of life; their inner focus is on the components and the attributes that attend this skill; their manner is in itself a demonstration of skill, of fine craftsmanship, of a control of language for austere poetic purposes. Murphy avoids what he sees as the quality of incantation or ritual in Yeats's poetry, preferring 'poetry which is an accurate memory of the tribe, of the people; a way of preserving the truth about the past.' 'Sailing to an Island' has this documentary quality. It is an objective narrative in which the consciousness of the observer is held in strict detachment. The emotional level is deliberate and cool. 'The Last Galway Hooker' is saved from cold objectivity by the warmth of the narrative, by the virtues it celebrates, above all by the connecting focus of attention on the embodiment of virtues, the hooker herself. Through a series of triumphs and failures, the progress is towards a conclusion in which past history is accumulated, and toward the renewal of virtues in craft — sailmaker, boatwright, steersman, their interrupted work resumed.

There is an elemental quality in many of Murphy's poems of the sea; their kinship with Anglo-Saxon voyages, contests, laments, seascapes and hazards is not merely a matter of four stressed lines as in 'The Last Galway Hooker'. The sea is a pleasure ground because it can bring the exhilaration of freedom, the testing of the self, and then the imaginative recovery of such experience in words. 'I'll tell the truth' the narrator says in 'Pat Cloherty's Version of *The Maisie*' and he does so, succinctly, clearly, unemotionally but with such fidelity, and such a persuasive use of oral techniques, that the impact is direct.

Murphy's delight in landscapes is evident in his most ambitious poem, 'The Battle of Aughrim', written between 1962 and 1967. Once again the concern is with the complex web of history which he approaches in a factual, demythologising manner. The poem places the past in perspective through a variety of incidents and attitudes before, during and after the battle. The battle itself is the focal point. On the one side is the responsiveness of the poet, on the other the far from dead matter of the past. The 'happening' is a result of this interaction of forces. The 'beginning' is in his blood, in the sense of heritage, because his ancestors were on both sides in this important battle. The poet takes his beginnings from it, since it shaped his destiny in the sense of class and religion; a beginning also in the now of the poem, in the poet's awakened response, beginning in the word. The opening question, 'Who owns the land...? ', raises issues about land ownership, about imaginative possession, about actual ownership now, and about the way in which a contemporary landscape yields up a reading of the past. One answer is – the poet. Throughout the whole first section he reveals his power of dual perception: the contemporary scene and within it and on equal terms with it, the past. That overlapping, dual vision determines the method of the poem, which is less a narrative than a series of individual vignettes that mirror each other to a variety of effects. Throughout, equations in the political, sectarian, social, religious and cultural areas play with and against each other through the poem's several voices, which in themselves are distinctive accents of race and class. The poem works through major contrasts and parallels in its four Parts, and through similar patterns between sections and within them.

Richard Murphy's response to words, to their sound, meaning, etymology, and texture, is particularly noticeable in *High Island* (1974). In 'Nocturne', almost an exercise in onomatopeia, the cries and signals of the petrels are echoed in the sounds and stresses. In 'Stormpetrel' he plays with words to suggest the quick movements of the birds and brings in archaic, dialect and colloquial terms. In 'Seals at High Island' he recreates the movements of tide and mammal. A number of poems in this collection, 'The Writing Lesson', 'The Reading Lesson' and 'Coppersmith', call attention to the problems of language, the difficulties of expression, and the relationship between language and identity. Contrasting dictions sometimes reinforce social, cultural or interpersonal differences.

To the wildness of the Irish tradition, as he sees it, Murphy brings his urge to impose order. His work attests his loyalty to his Ascendancy background, since that tradition survives in its ordered lines and civilised procedures. But he knows the risks: when you tame wild creatures, you make them vulnerable. Wildness itself is a virtue and should be respected and this principle animates the poetry of *High Island*. Throughout there is a respect for the world of nature, for the seals and the petrels, for their freedom and grace, which the poet records and to which he bears witness.

The issue of the 'Irishness' of his work was not central for Thomas
Kinsella. His early poetry owes more to Auden and the English
tradition in general, in themes as well as in techniques and conventions,
than it does to Yeats and in time, when the question was put to him,
he found the Irish tradition peculiarly broken. His early poetry is
notable for its lyric grace and music. 'Midsummer' delights in the play
of sound, in the musical and verbal possibilities of language. But it is
uncharacteristic. 'Baggot Street Deserta' is more typical, because of the
grave manner, the intelligent control, the specific setting, the touch of
self-deprecation, and the range to which it aspires. It is also one of
several poems in which the artistic act itself is the major concern. For
while Kinsella has for much of his poetic career been deeply aware,
even depressively concerned, with erosion, suffering and death, he has
been able to counter them by poetry itself. Thus 'The Laundress' is
an idealised portrait of a woman for whom these are not disturbing.
She finds fulfilment in a harmonious relationship with nature. But
'Cover Her Face' deals directly with death. It registers its impact in the
shocked, numbed response of the speaker, in the bewilderment of the
family, in its absorption of the details of the drab setting. 'Landscape
and Figure' presents life and death as inseparable and interchangeable.
The 'figure' is part of a natural order, of an evolutionary process in
which both forces have a part. In this poem the depressive elements,
so drably realised in 'Cover Her Face', where there are no consoling
features, are balanced by the belief that there is a creative, synthesizing
forward motion: 'Stalks still break into scattered flower./Tissue forms
about purpose as about seed'.

Kinsella sees the poet, in 'Baggot Street Deserta', 'The Secret
Garden' and other poems, as a person living in the forefront of the
evolutionary advance. 'The Secret Garden' is a vision poem that
illuminates the nature of existence, as he sees it. Tending the garden is
a momentary stay against destruction. Innocence and beauty exist, but
the total picture also contains dust and death.

The long *Nightwalker* poem (1967) has a significant place in
Kinsella's work, marking a decisive shift to poetry that is private and
inward in direction. Like *The Waste Land* it is made up of a series of
states of feeling within one figure. Its fluid narrative manner is similar
to the technique found in parts of *Ulysses,* in which there are also
apparently random associations of an individual consciousness. In its
material and setting it acknowledges Kinsella's appreciation of Joyce's
acceptance of the here and the now as subject-matter.

The poem is specifically Irish in its immediate contexts, as well as
being personal and autobiographical in some respects, but its

connecting theme is the violence inherent in modern life. This is projected through the walker who responds to his immediate surroundings in the Sandycove area of Dublin, close to Joyce's martello tower, and to the memories and associations that rise to the surface of his mind. In contexts that are generally apathetic, his consciousness is the active force. He accepts all that he encounters in the belief that through such patient and honest perception and apprehension he discovers meaning. The walker's anguish is intensified between the deceiving simplicities of education and his own actual experience, between Government pretensions and actual policies, between pseudo-nationalism and actual cultural loss. He suffers from a feeling of violence and betrayal done to himself and to his generation. To portray this sense of the gulf between appearance and reality the poem relies on a configuration of contrasting and related elements; a seemingly random assembly of incidents produces a meaningful pattern. And when the focus shifts to the lunar landscape, the reality is only marginally different from what has been seen on earth: sterility and evil there reflect in a radical and unambiguous fashion what the walker has experienced here.

'Hen Woman', 'Tear' and 'Sacrifice' come from *Notes from the Land of the Dead* (1973). 'Hen Woman' creates a moment of heightened and memorable apprehension. It is characteristic of the poems of encounter in this collection that the two central figures, of boy and grandmother, do not communicate; each tends to concentrate on his or her experience. The real concern of these poems, and 'Sacrifice' is an affirmation of this, is with the process and means of growth. Those that bring together child and grandmother establish the polarity of youth and age, innocence and experience. What the child finds in her, could he but digest all she represents, is his own future; she is his source of knowledge by virtue of her capacity to endure and absorb to the verge of death, to the edge of darkness and nothingness. 'Sacrifice' is an ecstatic celebration of union and possession, the full predatory penetration of another, the total fulfilment by means of another. Kinsella's perceptions of embryonic processes of growth are as intense as Kavanagh's natural supernaturalism. His discovery of living entities deep within the psyche is another affirmation of his faith in the natural forward movement which he sees in the language of the natural scientist, in 'Crab Orchard Sanctuary: Late October'. This poem unites his pleasure in beauties of the autumnal setting with regret for their passing. Given the familiar threat of erosion and decay at the heart of things, he can register the Darwinian density of nature with precision and clarity.

Finistère (1972) is an affirmation of man's hunger for new experience and a celebration of his creative spirit. The instinct that propels the travellers from Brittany to the Boyne Valley is a principle of discovery and creation. That sense of possibility, of an activating and positive instinct is inherent in much of Kinsella's poetry. The poem based on Jung's memoirs is another recognition of hidden impulses, of the 'alien garrison' of 'Baggot Street Deserta'.

John Montague has also been concerned with the contexts of Irish life. 'A Welcoming Party' reveals one side of his aspirations: a straining against the limitations of life in a small island, fearing its effects on his poetry; his yearning to be part of the European and universal context. At the same time he is concerned with the identification of those forces that have helped to shape his relationship with Ireland, with his own immediate Northern background, with the ways and customs of the people who live in the surroundings of his own home, with their lost and vanishing culture. Where Murphy explores the Ascendancy, Anglo-Irish ancestry, Montague explores the native, Catholic, peasant origins and his own family. One of the impulses these poets have in common particularly in recent years, is to be drawn back to the past, to places, people and events that link them psychically with the patterns of life, the cultural ambience, that have helped to shape their minds and imaginations. In dealing with the past Montague sketches out a mythic, pre-historic hinterland in a poem such as 'Like Dolmens Round my Childhood' where the old people are brought into line with the megalith makers. At the root of these poems that investigate his past is an attempt to unite his personal imagination and experiences with those of the community. Alienated from the region of his childhood, as Kavanagh was from Monaghan, he would repossess it imaginatively. Part of his technique is to allow literal details their proper fullness in poems that move slowly over the childhood world. Such poetry is an act of belief in the validity of that world.

The long sequence of poems, *The Rough Field*, is an ambitious return in this fashion to the parish of Garvaghey through which and within which Montague can recreate the lineaments of the recent and remote past, the personal and the familial, the historical and the mythical. The poem is both an expression of love for that small familiar world and a lament for its destruction by the forces of history, social change and modern progress. As in 'Nightwalker', there is a general and complex loss of landscape, of culture, of language, with the distinction that the speaker in *The Rough Field* returns to the childhood scene and leaves again.

The other large area of concern in Montague's work is that of love.

Some of his love poems have the quality of certain paintings: the details observed and precisely placed to form a total picture. The movement in the poem is towards a luminous revelation achieved through the coherence of its elements. At his best in the lyric form, Montague's concept of love takes in the complex nature of the relationship between men and women — love, pain, regret, the angelic and the sensual, the mystery of it all. In a poem called 'A Bright Day', he states his poetic aim — to express things as clearly and luminously as possible 'ritualizing the details', He seeks 'a slow exactness', The poem 'A Chosen Light' is a series of metaphors for this poetic aim. 'The low-pitched style', as he observes in another poem, 'seeks exactness, / Daring only to name the event'. In the love poems, in particular, this precision of language and of rhythm can be finely effective. In 'All Legendary Obstacles' where he tries to express the felt nature of the experience, but indirectly — in keeping with the inarticulate feelings of the lovers themselves — he also conveys suggestions of the archetypal, and of menace, with the result that the poem's potential is deeper than its actual, literal meanings.

Closely allied to the love poems are those of tender concern and of compassion for human beings. In 'Courtyard in Winter', the 'news' he brings is of 'sadness' and the belief that from 'bitter failure memory grows'. The elegiac mood recurs in some of the love poems, such as 'Herbert Street Revisited'. The trust in man's ability to endure is also a recurrent motif, as in 'The Point' and 'Edge'. Montague's work is also characterised by a sensuous feeling for nature. This quality is present in 'Woodtown Manor', in the particulars of 'A Severed Head'. In 'The Wild Dog Rose', in which there is once again the growth of understanding and compassion, the details of place, person and event provide a persuasive sense of actuality. The use of the image of the dog-rose to evoke the frail, persisting beauty of the old woman is just one of a number of occasions in which Montague makes effective metaphorical use of a natural object.

Like Patrick Kavanagh, Seamus Heaney draws his strength from the land. Respecting the crafts and skills of the countryside his early poems are themselves tidy and well-knit, bound by assonance, consonance and rhyme. They demonstrate a relationship, illuminating the forces that have shaped the poetic self. But they do more than describe and recreate. 'At a Potato Digging' begins like another description of Maguire and his men in 'The Great Hunger', but connects through the continuity of farm activities with the Great Famine and human disaster. Objective description leads to something ritualistic and primordial. The earth itself is 'the black / Mother'. The sod is 'a seasonal altar'. Potatoes become archaeological deposits: 'live skulls, blind-eyed'. Beyond the

some of Montague's work as an intermediate stage in this development. Clarke's distancing and low-keyed approach, similar to Murphy's in some respects, or to Kinsella's in the use of concrete particulars, is characteristic of his period, just as Heaney's tendency to merge with or absorb material is characteristic of his.

Throughout the poetry certain issues, emphases and responses are dominant. While philosophy and politics are not central, although they figure in Clarke, Devlin and Kinsella, tradition and individual growth are. The theme of growth is at the heart of Clarke, Kavanagh and Devlin and their successors are also concerned with it. Murphy's need for accurate recording of event and for precise locations are indicative of the need to place and define the self. Topographical emphasis in Murphy, Kavanagh, Heaney, Devlin and others is characteristic of Irish poetry as a whole. Kinsella's preoccupation with the processes of growth includes artistic growth, psychic myth and a Jungian sense of the subconscious. Heaney's layered vision frees him from exact chronology. His belief that the Irish psyche hoards memories also has a Jungian basis. The theme of love, as found in Montague and Devlin, is associated with that of growth, with understanding of the self and its relationships with others. In Kinsella love poems relate specifically to artistic growth which love helps to make possible. Sexuality enters positively into the poetry of Montague and Heaney, but in a more negative way, as a deprivation or an absence in Kavanagh. In Clarke it is associated at first with guilt, then with demonstrations of emotional liberation. It is remarkable how many poems are written about family figures: Clarke's portrait of Martha Blake, Montague's accounts of old women, Kinsella's of parents and grandparents, Heaney's 'Digging', and Murphy's 'The Woman of the House'. An elegiac strain runs through a number of these, combined sometimes with commemoration of the figures as embodiments of certain values or attributes. Religion in an orthodox sense figures in Clarke and Devlin, and to a lesser degree in Kavanagh, but by Heaney's time there is a different place of pilgrimage. Finally, as might be expected in a predominantly rural country, nature has an important place in virtually every poet.

The concept of tradition, as an actual entity, to be drawn upon, to be extended, deepened or reinterpreted, is also central. At times poets see it as threatened by the contemporary, by the secularization of thought, the spread of cities, the disruptions of rural and communal life, industrialization, and by the effects of progress. The tendency then is to lament the losses suffered, to commemorate past ways of life, particular individuals, a vanishing language, a culture under stress, to assert the resources of a distinctive culture in the face of pressures from the outside. The contrary impulse is to reject or condemn the forces that cause disruption and diminishments. A more positive response is to celebrate continuity, of the sub-culture of the small farms, of the life-ways of the countryside, of the western seaboard, or of particular figures. Poets who translate from the Irish, edit anthologies, or write critical articles about the literature are involved in the maintenance of tradition, in its re-assessment and strengthening. That kind of active, positive engagement with tradition characterised much of the career of Austin Clarke, who was deeply involved with the Irish heritage in the widest sense.

The ways in which poets respond to tradition vary. Clarke eventually faced up to the problems of conscience and single-handedly deepened and renewed our sense of the Irish heritage. Kavanagh dismissed the notion of Culture and enjoyed the habitual instead. Devlin turned his religious and emotional needs into a poetry in which the rhythms and idioms were expressive of his sensitive and intellectual personality. The diminishments of the Irish heritage, a constant factor throughout the modern period, results in two major directions: the extensions outward into European and other cultures and the extensions backward into the Irish past. Both reactions are attempts to nourish and strengthen the contemporary scene by compensating for its deficiencies and losses. The result in recent years is a more positive and more unfettered play of the intelligence and of the imagination as the poets alternate easily and unselfconsciously between Irish and non-Irish traditions.

AUSTIN CLARKE
(1896-1974)

PILGRIMAGE

When the far south glittered
Behind the grey beaded plains,
And cloudier ships were bitted
Along the pale waves,
The showery breeze — that plies
A mile from Ara — stood
And took our boat on sand:
There by dim wells the women tied
A wish on thorn, while rainfall
Was quiet as the turning of books
In the holy schools at dawn.

Grey holdings of rain
Had grown less with the fields,
As we came to that blessed place
Where hail and honey meet.
O Clonmacnoise was crossed
With light: those cloistered scholars,
Whose knowledge of the gospel
Is cast as metal in pure voices,
Were all rejoicing daily,
And cunning hands with cold and jewels
Brought chalices to flame.

Loud above the grassland,
In Cashel of the towers,
We heard with the yellow candles
The chanting of the hours,
White clergy saying High Mass,
A fasting crowd at prayer,
A choir that sang before them:
And in stained glass the holy day
Was sainted as we passed
Beyond that chancel where the dragons
Are carved upon the arch.

Treasured with chasuble,
Sun-braided, rich cloak'd wine-cup,
We saw, there, iron handbells,
Great annals in the shrine

A high-king bore to battle:
Where, from the branch of Adam,
The noble forms of language—
Brighter than green or blue enamels
Burned in white bronze—embodied
The wings and fiery animals
Which veil the chair of God.

Beyond a rocky townland
And that last tower where ocean
Is dim as haze, a sound
Of wild confession rose:
Black congregations moved
Around the booths of prayer
To hear a saint reprove them;
And from his boat he raised a blessing
To souls that had come down
The holy mountain of the west
Or wailed still in the cloud.

Light in the tide of Shannon
May ride at anchor half
The day and, high in spar-top
Or leather sails of their craft,
Wine merchants will have sleep;
But on a barren isle,
Where Paradise is praised
At daycome, smaller than the sea-gulls,
We heard white Culdees pray
Until our hollow ship was kneeling
Over the longer waves.

NIGHT AND MORNING

I know the injured pride of sleep,
The strippers at the mocking-post,
The insult in the house of Caesar
And every moment that can hold
In brief the miserable act
Of centuries.Thought can but share
Belief—and the tormented soul,
Changing confession to despair,
Must wear a borrowed robe.

Morning has moved the dreadful candle,
Appointed shadows cross the nave,
Unlocked by the secular hand,
The very elements remain
Appearances upon the altar.
Adoring priest has turned his back
Of gold upon the congregation.
All saints have had their day at last,
But thought still lives in pain.

How many councils and decrees
Have perished in the simple prayer
That gave obedience to the knee;
Trampling of rostrum, feathering
Of pens at cock-rise, sum of reason
To elevate a common soul:
Forgotten as the minds that bled
For us, the miracle that raised
A language from the dead.

O when all Europe was astir
With echo of learned controversy,
The voice of logic led the choir.
Such quality was in all being,
The forks of heaven and this earth
Had met, town-walled, in mortal view
And in the pride that we ignore,
The holy rage of argument,
God was made man once more.

TENEBRAE

This is the hour that we must mourn
With tallows on the black triangle,
Night has a napkin deep in fold
To keep the cup; yet who dare pray
If all in reason should be lost,
The agony of man betrayed
At every station of the cross?

O when the forehead is too young,
Those centuries of mortal anguish,
Dabbed by a consecrated thumb

That crumbles into dust, will bring
Despair with all that we can know;
And there is nothing left to sing,
Remembering our innocence.

I hammer on that common door,
Too frantic in my superstition,
Transfix with nails that I have broken,
The angry notice of the mind.
Close as the thought that suffers him,
The habit every man in time
Must wear beneath his ironed shirt.

An open mind disturbs the soul,
And in disdain I turn my back
Upon the sun that makes a show
Of half the world, yet still deny
The pain that lives within the past,
The flame sinking upon the spike,
Darkness that man must dread at last.

THE STRAYING STUDENT

On a holy day when sails were blowing southward,
A bishop sang the Mass at Inishmore,
Men took one side, their wives were on the other
But I heard the woman coming from the shore:
And wild in despair my parents cried aloud
For they saw the vision draw me to the doorway.

Long had she lived in Rome when Popes were bad,
The wealth of every age she makes her own,
Yet smiled on me in eager admiration,
And for a summer taught me all I know,
Banishing shame with her great laugh that rang
As if a pillar caught it back alone.

I learned the prouder counsel of her throat,
My mind was growing bold as light in Greece;
And when in sleep her stirring limbs were shown,
I blessed the noonday rock that knew no tree:
And for an hour the mountain was her throne,
Although her eyes were bright with mockery.

They say I was sent back from Salamanca
And failed in logic, but I wrote her praise
Nine times upon a college wall in France.
She laid her hand at darkfall on my page
That I might read the heavens in a glance
And I knew every star the Moors have named.

Awake or in my sleep, I have no peace now,
Before the ball is struck, my breath has gone,
And yet I tremble lest she may deceive me
And leave me in this land, where every woman's son
Must carry his own coffin and believe,
In dread, all that the clergy teach the young.

PENAL LAW

Burn Ovid with the rest. Lovers will find
A hedge-school for themselves and learn by heart
All that the clergy banish from the mind,
When hands are joined and head bows in the dark.

CELEBRATIONS

Who dare complain or be ashamed
Of liberties our arms have taken?
For every spike upon that gateway,
We have uncrowned the past:
And open hearts are celebrating
Prosperity of church and state
In the shade of Dublin Castle.

So many flagpoles can be seen now
Freeing the crowd, while crisscross keys,
On yellow-and-white above the green,
Treble the wards of nation,
God only knows what treasury
Uncrams to keep each city borough
And thoroughfare in grace.

Let ageing politicians pray
Again, hoardings recount our faith,
The blindfold woman in a rage
Condemns her own for treason:
No steeple topped the scale that Monday,
Rebel souls had lost their savings
And looters braved the street.

ANCIENT LIGHTS

When all of us wore smaller shoes
And knew the next world better than
The knots we broke, I used to hurry
On missions of my own to Capel
Street, Bolton Street and Granby Row
To see what man has made. But darkness
Was roomed with fears. Sleep, stripped by woes
I had been taught, beat door, leaped landing,
Lied down the bannisters of naught.

Being sent to penance, come Saturday,
I shuffled slower than my sins should.
My fears were candle-spiked at side-shrines,
Rays lengthened them in stained-glass. Confided
To night again, my grief bowed down.
Heard hand on shutter-knob. Did I
Take pleasure, when alone—how much—
In a bad thought, immodest look
Or worse, unnecessary touch?

Closeted in the confessional,
I put on flesh, so many years
Were added to my own, attempted
In vain to keep Dominican
As much i' the dark as I was, mixing
Whispered replies with his low words;
Then shuddered past the crucifix,
The feet so hammered, daubed-on blood-drip,
Black with lip-scrimmage of the damned.

Once as I crept from the church-steps,
Beside myself, the air opened
On purpose. Nature read in a flutter
An evening lesson above my head.
Atwirl beyond the leadings, corbels,
A cage-bird came among sparrows
(The moral inescapable)
Plucked, roof-mired, all in mad bits. O
The pizzicato of its wires!

Goodness of air can be proverbial:
That day, by the kerb at Rutland Square,
A bronze bird fabled out of trees,
Mailing the spearheads of the railings,
Sparrow at nails. I hailed the skies
To save the tiny dropper, found
Appetite gone. A child of clay
Had blustered it away. Pity
Could raise some littleness from dust.

What Sunday clothes can change us now
Or humble orders in black and white?
Stinking with centuries the act
Of thought. So think, man, as Augustine
Did, dread the ink-bespattered ex-monk,
And keep your name. No, let me abandon
Night's jakes. Self-persecuted of late
Among the hatreds of rent Europe,
Poetry burns at a different stake.

Still, still I remember aweful downpour
Cabbing Mountjoy Street, spun loneliness
Veiling almost the Protestant church,
Two backyards from my very home,
I dared to shelter at locked door.
There, walled by heresy, my fears
Were solved. I had absolved myself:
Feast-day effulgence, as though I gained
For life a plenary indulgence.

The sun came out, new smoke flew up,
The gutters of the Black Church rang
With services. Waste water mocked
The ballcocks: down-pipes sparrowing,
And all around the spires of Dublin
Such swallowing in the air, such cowling
To keep high offices pure: I heard
From shore to shore, the iron gratings
Take half our heavens with a roar.

THE ENVY OF POOR LOVERS

Pity poor lovers who may not do what they please
With their kisses under a hedge, before a raindrop
Unhouses it; and astir from wretched centuries,
Bramble and briar remind them of the saints.

Her envy is the curtain seen at night-time,
Happy position that could change her name.
His envy—clasp of the married whose thoughts can
      be alike,
Whose nature flows without the blame or shame.

Lying in the grass as if it were a sin
To move, they hold each other's breath, tremble,
Ready to share that ancient dread—kisses begin
Again—of Ireland keeping company with them.

Think, children, of institutions mured above
Your ignorance, where every look is veiled,
State-paid to snatch away the folly of poor lovers
For whom, it seems, the sacraments have failed.

USUFRUCT

This house cannot be handed down.
Before the scriven ink is brown,
Clergy will sell the lease of it.
I live here, thinking, ready to flit
From Templeogue, but not at ease.
I hear the flood unclay the trees,
Road-stream of traffic. So does the midge,

With myriads below the bridge,
Having his own enormous day,
Unswallowed. Ireland was never lay.
My mother wore no rural curch
Yet left her savings to the Church,
That she might aid me by-and-by,
Somewhere beyond the threatening sky.
What could she do, if such in faith
Be second nature? A blue wraith
That exquisites the pool, I mean
The kingfisher, too seldom seen,
Is warier than I am. Flash
Of inspiration makes thought rash.

MISS MARNELL

No bells rang in her house. The silver plate
Was gone. She scarcely had a candle-wick,
Though old, to pray by, ne'er a maid to wait
At all. She had become a Catholic
So long ago, we smiled, did good by stealth,
Bade her good-day, invited her to tea
With deep respect. Forgetting her loss of wealth,
She took barmbrack and cake so hungrily,
We pitied her, wondered about her past.
But her poor mind had not been organized;
She was taken away, fingering to the last
Her ivory decades. Every room surprised:
Wardrobes of bombazine, silk dresses, stank:
Cobwebby shrouds, pantries, cupboard, bone-bare.
Yet she had prospering money in the bank,
Admiring correspondents everywhere,
In Ireland, Wales, the Far East, India;
Her withered hand was busy doing good
Against our older missions in Africa.
False teeth got little acid from her food:
But scribble helped to keep much mortar wet
For convent, college, higher institution,
To build new churches or reduce their debt.
The figure on her cross-cheque made restitution
For many sins. Piled on her escritoire

Were necessary improvements, paint-pot, ladder
And new coats from Maynooth, in a world at war,
Circulars, leaflets, pleas that made her madder
To comfort those who need for holy living
Their daily post: litterings, flyblown, miced
In corners, faded notes of thanksgiving,
All signed—'Yours Gratefully, In Jesus Christ.'

THE LOSS OF STRENGTH

Farm-brooks that come down to Rathfarnham
By grange-wall, tree-stop, from the hills,
Might never have heard the rustle in barn dance,
The sluicing, bolting, of their flour-mills,
Nor have been of use in the steady reel
On step-boards of the iron wheel-rim,
For Dublin crowds them in: they wheeze now
Beneath new pavements, name old laneways,
Discharge, excrete, their centuries,
Man-trapped in concrete, deeper drainage.
Yet, littling by itself, I found one
That had never run to town.

No artificial fly or wet-hook
Could stickle it. Summer was cressing
Her mats, an inch from reeds. The brooklet
Ran clearly under bramble. Dressed
In the newest of feathers, black, trimmed
With white, a pair of waterhens dimmed
Away from me, with just a dot
Of red. Three visitors, one soul
Among them or not. Know-all can tot it
Up. Lesser bits of life console us:
Nature at jest in light and shade,
Though somewhat afraid.

I climb among the hills no more
To taste a last water, hide in cloud-mist
From sheep and goat: The days are downpour.
Cycle is gone, warm patch on trousers.
All, all, drive faster, stink without,
Spirit and spark within, no doubt.

When hope was active, I stood taller
Than my own sons. Beloved strength
Springs past me, three to one. Halldoor
Keeps open, estimates the length
To which I go: a mile to tire-a.
But I knew the stone beds of Ireland.

Beclipped and confident of shank,
I rode the plain with chain that freed me.
On a rim akin to air, I cranked up
Standstill of gradient, freewheeled
Down glens beyond our national school,
Our catechism and British rule,
To find, thought I, the very roc's nest
A-spar on Diamond Hill; clouted
By wind, strawing the narrowest sea-lough,
A speck that saw a cloud put out
A goose-neck, counting far below
The Twelve Pins in a row.

The young must have a solitude
To feel the strength in mind, restore
Small world of liking. Saints have spewed
Too much. I wanted test of stories
Our poets had talked about, pinmeal
To potboil long ago. Cloud-feelers
Featherers, touched our restlessness.
Lost prosody restrained us. Summit
Showed valleys, reafforesting,
The Fianna, leaf-veined, among them.
Now only a wishing-cap could leave me
On the top of Slieve Mish.

Shannoning from the tide, a sea-god
Became our servant once, demeaned
Himself, a three-legged, slippery body:
Uncatchable, being submarine,
He spoked the hub. Now engineering
Machinery destroys the weirs,
Directs, monk-like, our natural flow:
Yet it was pleasant at Castleconnell
To watch the salmon brighten their raincoats.
The reeds wade out for what is gone:
That mile of spray faraway on the rapids
Is hidden in a tap.

My childish dreams were devildom.
Sleep rose and sank: the Great Flood waked me.
Reservoir at low level! Come,
Dear rain and save our Roundwood lake!
Should man complain of plans that curb
Torrent in turbine? Great disturbance:
The hush of light. Why keep with Fintan
The Falls of Assaroe, trample
Of transmigration, void of man
In shape of salmon? Those currents were ample.
Voltage has turned them, riddle and all,
To a piddle and blank wall.

Thousands ply the wonted scissors,
Cut up the immaterial, take
Our measure. When the soul is body-busy,
Rhyme interferes for its own sake
But gets no credit. Late in the day,
Then, coasting back from Milltown Malbay,
I saw before bell rang a warning,
Scattery Island and its round tower.
A child was scorching by that corner
To hurl me back, unknottable power,
Hell-fire in twist and turn, grotesque:
Now, Celtic-Romanesque.

Abraham's Bosom was a coldness.
My companies got up from dust
In meditation. Granite unfolded
The Gospel, figured speech. Must bowed
To Shall in our Jerusalem:
Saintly acquaintance. John o' the Bosom
Inspired our quiet. Young disciples
Did their own field and house work: no women
Tattling, no infants there to wipe
And scold. Yet Devil mocked at hymnal:
His smoke annoyed our Kevin, itched
Heavenly nose in kitchen.

Celibacy is our best rule still,
Restraint increasing its adherents.
Stuck-honey embitters. Though the schoolmen
Denounce our senses, what can fear add?
Let women masculate with hair-cuts,

Piety hates their very guts
But makes no comment on what shortens.
Refrain, poor sight, for much goes bare:
Walking temptations, visible mortal
Sins, churched by fashion. Fewer stare now.
Layman watches the theológian,
Both, us. A cogent clan.

Too long near London, I broke in exile
Another bread. The nightingales
Naturalised my own vexation:
Yet, dearer on Inish Caltra, one boat-hail
At dawn. Their Cummin learned to hum
Angelic breves and found the Thummim.
Illuminative centre, arc
By arc was circumscribed. A field
Too small, perhaps, in truth: the skylark
May hatch out cuckoo. Thought shielded
Sunnier pen-stroke. No friend of Alcuin's,
I saw God's light through ruins.

Blessing of staves, a-hurry on wave-top,
You gave to Europe; isle of fair hills.
Cure now my ills. Scholars, who shaved
The forehead, were often up in air,
Beatifying themselves by acts
Unrecognised at Rome. No pacts
With Nature diverted river, raised up
Lake. Miracles anticipated
Immoderate science of our days.
Clearly religion has never hated
A better world. Invention lies,
If truth can be surprised.

Too great a vine, they say, can sour
The best of clay. No pair of sinners
But learned saints had overpowered
Our country, Malachi the Thin
And Bernard of Clairvaux. Prodigious
In zeal, these cooled and burned our porridge.
(Later came breakspear, strong bow backing)
The arch sprang wide for their Cistercians.
O bread was wersh and well was brack.
War rattled at us in hammered shirts:
An Englishman had been the Pontiff.
They marched to Mellifont.

But time goes back. Monks, whom we praise now,
Take down a castle, stone by stone,
To make an abbey, restore the chain-light
Of silence. Gelignite has blown up
Too much: yet on the Hill of Allen,
The blasters are ·at work. Gallon
By gallon our roads go on. Stonecrushers
Must feed them. Fionn hunted here, Oisin
Complained of age. I think of rushed bones,
Bogland, in furnaces, grown greener,
The prophecy of Colmcille—
Car without horse—fulfilled.

Red, white and blue pegged up the pulley
When I ran to school, ready to snatch all,
Buckle and satchel. Holier colours
Look down. Our Easter Rising—a scratch
In empire, self-wounded by war and truce.
Last night, as if the screws were loose,
I heard high over Whitefriar Street
Din of a flyer, may be *St. Kevin,*
St. Brigid or *St. Brendan.* Greeting
To overheads! Freedom will never
Rust here, as my poor pedal did.
Mould ran away with the medal.

See, faith and science reconciled:
Stepmother with child. Whispering of ward-screens,
Hope that no specialist has smiled on
Removes our corporal disorders.
Above the clouds where all is white
And blue, with nothing to alight on,
Annual pilgrimages, sprinkled
With blessings, go: flown hospitals.
Let Baily bow, Kish-i'-the-ship wink,
Poolbeg flash out to Rocklit-bill.
Through grottoes of cloud they come; few cured
At Lourdes: all reassured.

Loss but repeats the startling legend
Of time. A poet wants no more
To palliate his mind, edging
Worn cards behind a shaky door
Or tinting them until the puce

Shuffle the purple. May the Deuce
Take all of them and thought get better!
While faith and country play a far hand!
Plod on, tired rhyme. The streams that wetted
Forgotten wheels push past Rathfarnham,
Half underground: slime steps on stone,
I count them — not my own.

BURIAL OF AN IRISH PRESIDENT
(Dr. Douglas Hyde)

The tolling from St. Patrick's
Cathedral was brangled, repeating
Itself in top-back room
And alley of the Coombe, *(slum)*
Crowding the dirty streets,
Upbraiding all our pat tricks.
Tricoloured and beflowered,
Coffin of our President,
Where fifty mourners bowed,
Was trestled in the gloom
Of arch and monument,
Beyond the desperate tomb
Of Swift. Imperial flags,
Corunna, Quatre Bras,
Inkermann, Pretoria,
Their pride turning to rags,
Drooped, smoke-thin as the booming
Of cannon. The simple word
From heaven was vaulted, stirred
By candles. At the last bench
Two Catholics, the French
Ambassador and I, knelt down.
The vergers waited. Outside.
The hush of Dublin town,
Professors of cap and gown,
Costello, his Cabinet,
In Government cars, hiding
Around the corner, ready
Tall hat in hand, dreading
Our Father in English. Better
Not hear that 'which' for 'who'
And risk eternal doom.

MARTHA BLAKE AT FIFTY-ONE

Early, each morning, Martha Blake
    Walked, angeling the road,
To Mass in the Church of the Three Patrons.
    Sanctuary lamp glowed
And the clerk halo'ed the candles
    On the High Altar. She knelt
Illumined. In gold-hemmed alb,
    The priest intoned. Wax melted.

Waiting for daily Communion, bowed head
    At rail, she hears a murmur.
Latin is near. In a sweet cloud
    That cherub'd, all occurred.
The voice went by. To her pure thought,
    Body was a distress
And soul a sigh. Behind her denture,
    Love lay, a helplessness.

Then, slowly walking after Mass
    Down Rathgar Road, she took out
Her Yale key, put a match to gas-ring,
    Half filled a saucepan, cooked
A fresh egg lightly, with tea, brown bread,
    Soon, taking off her blouse
And skirt, she rested, pressing the Crown
    Of Thorns until she drowsed.

In her black hat, stockings, she passed
    Nylons to a nearby shop
And purchased, daily, with downcast eyes,
    Fillet of steak or a chop.
She simmered it on a low jet,
    Having a poor appetite,
Yet never for an hour felt better
    From dilatation, tightness.

She suffered from dropped stomach, heartburn
    Scalding, water-brash
And when she brought her wind up, turning
    Red with the weight of mashed
Potato, mint could not relieve her.
    In vain her many belches,
For all below was swelling, heaving
    Wamble, gurgle, squelch.

She lay on the sofa with legs up,
   A decade on her lip,
At four o'clock, taking a cup
   Of lukewarm water, sip
By sip, but still her daily food
   Repeated and the bile
Tormented her. In a blue hood,
   The Virgin sadly smiled

When she looked up, the Saviour showed
   His Heart, daggered with flame
And, from the mantle-shelf, St. Joseph
   Bent, disapproving. Vainly
She prayed for in the whatnot corner,
   The new Pope was frowning. Night
And day, dull pain, as in her corns,
   Recounted every bite.

She thought of St. Teresa, floating
   On motes of a sunbeam,
Carmelite with scatterful robes,
   Surrounded by demons,
Small black boys in their skin. She gaped
   At Hell: a muddy passage
That led to nothing, queer in shape,
   A cupboard closely fastened.

Sometimes, the walls of the parlour
   Would fade away. No plod
Of feet, rattle of van, in Garville
   Road. Soul now gone abroad
Where saints, like medieval serfs,
   Had laboured. Great sun-flower shone.
Our Lady's Chapel was borne by seraphs,
   Three leagues beyond Ancona.

High towns of Italy, the plain
   Of France, were known to Martha
As she read in a holy book. The sky-blaze
   Nooned at Padua,
Marble grotto of Bernadette.
   Rose-scatterers. New saints
In tropical Africa where the tsetse
   Fly probes, the forest taints.

Teresa had heard the Lutherans
    Howling on red-hot spit,
And grill, men who had searched for truth
    Alone in Holy Writ.
So Martha, fearful of flame lashing
    Those heretics, each instant,
Never dealt in the haberdashery
    Shop, owned by two Protestants.

In ambush of night, an angel wounded
    The Spaniard to the heart
With iron tip on fire. Swooning
    With pain and bliss as a dart
Moved up and down within her bowels
    Quicker, quicker, each cell
Sweating as if rubbed up with towels,
    Her spirit rose and fell.

St. John of the Cross, her friend, in prison
    Awaits the bridal night,
Paler than lilies, his wizened skin
    Flowers. In fifths of flight,
Senses beyond seraphic thought,
    In that divinest clasp,
Enfolding of kisses that cauterize,
    Yield to the soul-spasm.

Cunning in body had come to hate
    All this and stirred by mischief
Haled Martha from heaven. Heart palpitates
    And terror in her stiffens.
Heart misses one beat, two... flutters... stops.
    Her ears are full of sound.
Half fainting, she stares at the grandfather clock
    As if it were overwound.

The fit had come. Ill-natured flesh
    Despised her soul. No bending
Could ease rib. Around her heart, pressure
    Of wind grew worse. Again,
Again, armchaired without relief,
    She eructated, phlegm
In mouth, forgot the woe, the grief,
    Foretold at Bethlehem.

Tired of the same faces, side-altars,
    She went to the Carmelite Church
At Johnson's Court, confessed her faults,
    There, once a week, purchased
Tea, butter in Chatham St. The pond
    In St. Stephen's Green was grand.
She watched the seagulls, ducks, black swan,
    Went home by the 15 tram.

Her beads in hand, Martha became
    A member of the Third Order,
Saved from long purgatorial pain,
    Brown habit and white cord
Her own when cerges had been lit
    Around her coffin. She got
Ninety-five pounds on loan for her bit
    Of clay in the common plot.

Often she thought of a quiet sick-ward,
    Nuns, with delicious ways,
Consoling the miserable: quick
    Tea, toast on trays. Wishing
To rid themselves of her, kind neighbours
    Sent for the ambulance,
Before her brother and sister could hurry
    To help her. Big gate clanged.

No medical examination
    For the new patient. Doctor
Had gone to Cork on holidays.
    Telephone sprang. Hall-clock
Proclaimed the quarters. Clatter of heels
    On tiles. Corridor, ward,
A-whirr with the electric cleaner,
    The creak of window cord.

She could not sleep at night. Feeble
    And old, two women raved
And cried to God. She held her beads.
    O how could she be saved?
The hospital had this and that rule.
    Day-chill unshuttered. Nun, with
Thermometer in reticule,
    Went by. The women mumbled.

Mother Superior believed
That she was obstinate, self-willed.
Sisters ignored her, hands-in-sleeves,
Beside a pantry shelf
Or counting pillow-case, soiled sheet.
They gave her purgatives.
Soul-less, she tottered to the toilet.
Only her body lived.

Wasted by colitis, refused
The daily sacrament
By regulation, forbidden use
Of bed-pan, when meals were sent up,
Behind a screen, she lay, shivering,
Unable to eat. The soup
Was greasy, mutton, beef or liver,
Cold. Kitchen has no scruples.

The Nuns had let the field in front
As an Amusement Park,
Merry-go-round, a noisy month, all
Heltering-skeltering at darkfall,
Mechanical music, dipper, hold-tights,
Rifle-crack, crash of dodgems.
The ward, godless with shadow, lights,
How could she pray to God?

Unpitied, wasting with diarrhoea
And the constant strain,
Poor Child of Mary with one idea,
She ruptured a small vein,
Bled inwardly to jazz. No priest
Came. She had been anointed
Two days before, yet knew no peace:
Her last breath, disappointed.

JAPANESE PRINT

Both skyed
In south-west wind beyond
Poplar and fir-tree, swallow,
Heron, almost collide,
Swerve
With a rapid
Dip of wing, flap,
Each in an opposite curve,
Fork-tail, long neck outstretched
And feet. All happened
Above my head. The pair
Was disappearing. Say I
Had seen, half hint, a sketch on
Rice-coloured air,
Sharako, Hokusai!

CYPRESS GROVE

I
'Grob! Grob', goes the raven peering from his rift
Above Lough Bray, glimmer on eyelid, feather—
Shadow in water— sets out for Kippure
By upper Glencree, at morning, devil-dot
Above the last bog-cutting, hears the lark totting
And dips along gullies by the twig-drip of heather
Down to the pond-level, the steps of Bohernabreena,
Then winging over Seefin, takes the pure
Cold air — ravenous, searching — comes to that green
Bowl set among hills, Punchestown, its race-course
So often whiskeyed with the roar of crowd
Nearer, farther, as binoculars
Hastily swivel the Grand Stand, hoarser
Where black-red-violet-blue-white-yellow dots
Are hunched along the slope: backers from bars
And, shaded by huge umbrellas, bookmakers,
Are waving caps above the stalls. That hurly-burly
A mile away: he sees the pewter cloud
Above Church Mountain, past the double lake,
Flaps by the King's River, sandy spots:
Behind him the dairy farms — the acres tree'd,

Thin-streamed — then flies up where the gusts are blowing
Over the ceannavaun and nothing is showing,
Hidden awhile in vapouring of screes
'Ur! Ur', he croaks to himself, a flying speck
And turning northward over Annalecky
Where a man by the Slaney might stoop to hook a
Trout, play it, looks down into Poulaphouca.

II

At daybreak, hurrying home too late, by peel
And pale, goes Jack o'Lantern, turning on heel,
Jumping the bog-drain, last Elizabethan.
The raven sees the doublet of that trickster
Darting, like his own flame-spot underneath,
While shadowkins play among themselves at nix.
As early, the black fellow beaking along the Dodder,
Spies in a reedy pool the water-hen
Gliding behind the cress, a constant nodder,
Then mantles across the river to the fields,
The strippers half-asleep, where once the Spa
At Templeogue was fashionable, now wheel-less.
Hundreds of pigeons clap up from Cheeverstown,
Sink down again into the damp of the shaw.
He flies two miles by a gorse-budded glen
To a forgotten sandpit or a quarry
That leads the sheep to nowhere like a corrie,
Ironwork scraps, our twisted thoughts, unshacked,
Turns, seeing a single streak between the grass-mounds,
The paven conduit with an inch of ripple
That Normans drank in Dublin, centuries
Ago, provinces at their shaven lips.
It brims a stock-pond, hurries underground
By cellarage of an eighteenth-century mansion.
The sewered city with a rump of suburbs
Has reached the pillared gate in its expansion,
Design of the daffodils, the urns, disturbed by
Air-scrooging builders, men who buy and sell fast.
One Gallagher bought the estate. Now concrete-mixers
Vomit new villas: builder, they say, from Belfast
With his surveyors turning down the oil-wicks.
The shadow is going out from Cypress Grove,
The solemn branches echoing our groan,
Where open carriages, barouches, drove:
Walnut, rare corktree, torn up by machine.

I hear the shrills of the electric saw
Lopping the shelter, unsapping the winter-green
For wood-yards, miss at breakfast time the cawing
Of local rooks. Many have moved to Fortrose.
They hear in my lifted hand a gun-report,
Scatter their peace in another volley.
                                             . I stare:
Elegant past blown out like a torchère.

MNEMOSYNE LAY IN DUST

I
Past the house where he was got
In darkness, terrace, provision shop,
Wing-hidden convent opposite,
Past public-houses at lighting-up
Time, crowds outside them — Maurice Devane
Watched from the taxi window in vain
National stir and gaiety
Beyond himself: St. Patrick's Day,
The spike-ends of the Blue Coat school,
Georgian houses, ribald gloom
Rag-shadowed by gaslight, quiet pavements
        Moon-waiting in Blackhall Place.

For six weeks Maurice had not slept,
Hours pillowed him from right to left side,
Unconsciousness became the pit
Of terror. Void would draw his spirit,
Unself him. Sometimes he fancied that music,
Soft lights in Surrey, Kent, could cure him,
Hypnotic touch, until, one evening,
The death-chill seemed to mount from feet
To shin, to thigh. Life burning in groin
And prostate ached for a distant joy.
But nerves need solitary confinement.
        Terror repeals the mind.

Cabs ranked at Kingsbridge Station, Guinness
Tugs moored at their wooden quay, glinting
Of Liffey mudbank; hidden vats
Brewing intoxication, potstill,

Laddering of distilleries
Ready to sell their jollities,
Delirium tremens. Dublin swayed,
Drenching, drowning the shamrock: unsaintly
Mirth. The high departments were filed,
Yard, store, unlit. Whiskey-all-round,
Beyond the wealth of that square mile,
    Was healthing every round.

The eighteenth century hospital
Established by the tears of Madam
Steevens, who gave birth, people said, to
A monster with a pig's snout, pot-head.
The Ford turned right, slowed down. Gates opened,
Closed with a clang; acetylene glow
Of headlights. How could Maurice Devane
Suspect from weeping-stone, porch, vane,
The classical rustle of the harpies,
Hopping in filth among the trees,
The Mansion of Forgetfulness
    Swift gave us for a jest?

II
Straight-jacketing sprang to every lock
And bolt, shadowy figures shocked,
Wall, ceiling; hat, coat, trousers flung
From him, vest, woollens, Maurice was plunged
Into a steaming bath; half suffocated,
He sank, his assailants gesticulating,
A Keystone reel gone crazier;
The terror-peeling celluloid,
Whirling the figures into vapour,
    Dissolved them. All was void.

Drugged in the dark, delirious,
In vision Maurice saw, heard, struggle
Of men and women, shouting, groans.
In an accident at Westland Row,
Two locomotives with mangle of wheel-spokes,
Colliding: up-scatter of smoke, steel,
Above: the gong of ambulances.
Below, the quietly boiling hiss
Of steam, the winter-sleet of glances,
    The quiet boiling of pistons.

The crowds were noisy. Sudden cries
Of 'Murder! Murder!' from a byway,
The shriek of women with upswollen
Bodies, held down in torment, rolling
And giving birth to foundlings, shriek
After shriek, the blanket lifting unspeakable
Protrusions. The crowds were stumbling backward,
Barefooted cry of 'Murder' scurried.
Police batoned eyesight into blackness.
      Bandages were blurred.

Maurice had wakened up. He saw a
Circular peep-hole rimmed with polished
Brass within the door. It gloomed.
A face was glaring into the bed-room
With bulging eyes and fierce moustache.
Quicker than thought, a torchlight flashed
From wall to pillow. Motionless,
It spied until the face had gone.
The sound of sleepers in unrest:
      Still watchful, the peep-hole shone.

What night was it, he heard the creaking
Of boots and tiptoed to the peep-hole?
Four men were carrying a coffin
Upon their shoulders. As they shuffled,
Far in his mind a hollaloo
Echoed: 'The Canon of Killaloe...'
Death-chill would mount from feet to limbs,
His loins, secretion no longer burn.
Those shoulderers would come for him with
      The shroud, spade, last thud.

Nightly he watched a masquerade
Go by his cell and was afraid
Of one — the stooping, bald-headed madman
Who muttered curse after curse, his hands
Busily knitting, twiddling white reeds:
So huge, he seemed to be the leader.
The others tormented by their folly,
The narrows of the moon, crowded
Together, gibboned his gestures, followed
      That madman knitting reed, brow.

Once, getting out of bed, he peeped
Into the dormitory. Sheet
And slip were laundry-white. Dazes
Of electric light came down. Patients
Stirred fitfully. Their fidgeting marred
With scrawls the whiteness of the ward,
Gift of the moon. He wondered who
He was, but memory had hidden
All. Someone sat beside him, drew
        Chair nearer, murmured: 'Think!'

One afternoon, he looked in dread
Into the ward outside. The beds
Were empty. Quiet sunshine glowed
On waxed floor and brass. He hurried
Across to the high window, stood
On the hot pipes to see the view.
Below there was a widespread garden,
With shrubberies, walks, summerhouses.
He stared in wonder from his bars,
        Saddened by the boughs.

III
Men were looking up
        At the sky
As if they had lost something,
        They could not find.

Gesticulating by summerhouse,
        Shrubbery, side-path,
They wandered slowly, pallid dots,
        Faces gone blind.

Looking down from the bars
        With mournful eye
Maurice could see them beckoning,
        Some pointed, signed.

Waving their arms and hands,
        They wandered. Why
Should they pretend they did not see him,
        Lost to mind?

They walked to and fro
　　By shrubbery, side-path,
Gesticulating like foreigners
　　Or loitering behind.

But all were looking up
　　At the sky
As if they had lost something,
　　They could not find.

IV
Tall, handsome, tweeded Dr. Leeper
Inspecting the mindless at a glance
Quick-striding, always ready to leap,
A duffering Victorian;
The mad-eyed Dr. Rutherford,
　　Agreeable in word
And the Superintendent, Mr. Rhys,
That burly Welshman ready to pounce
From everywhere with his band of seizers,
　　Drug maniacs as they bounce.

One morning as he washed his face
And hands, he noticed that the basin
Was different: the soap-dish had
Been moved an inch. Was it a trap
To test his observation? Cuting,
He put it back, for he was sure
It was a spy. Yes, his suspicions
Were right. But would he not forget
Next day where he had moved the soap-dish,
What other trap his foes would set?

Often he stared into the mirror
Beside the window, hand-drawn by fear.
He seemed to know that bearded face
In it, the young man, tired and pale,
Half smiling. Gold-capped tooth in front
Vaguely reminded him of someone.
Who was it? Nothing came to him.
He saw that smile again. Gold dot
Still gleamed. The bearded face was drawn
With sufferings he had forgotten.

Sunlight was time. All day in a dream
He heard the quiet voice of steam,
Drowsy machinery, hurried
A student again. Class-books were stirring,
His footstep echoed by Grangegorman
Beneath the granite wall, enormous
Gate. Was it the Richmond Asylum? He pondered
Beneath the wall, still heard the hissing
And lisp of steam in the laundry
There, memory afoot, he listened.

Out of the morning came the buzzing
Of forest bees. The tiger muzzle
Gnarled as myriads of them bumbled
Heavily towards the jungle honey.
A sound of oriental greeting;
Ramàyana, Bhagavad-gita,
Hymnal of Brahma, Siva, Vishnu.
'The temple is gone. Where is the pather?'
A foolish voice in English said:
'He's praying to his little Father.'

Weakening, he lay flat. Appetite
Had gone. The beef or mutton, potatoes
And cabbage — he turned from the thick slices
Of meat, the greasy rings of gravy.
Knife had been blunted, fork was thick
And every plate was getting bigger.
His stomach closed: he eyed the food,
Disgusted: always beef or mutton,
Potatoes, cabbage, turnips. Mind spewed,
Only in dreams was gluttonous.

V
Maurice was in an Exhibition Hall
Where crowds of men and fashionable women
In bosoming dresses, embroidered shawl,
        Were moving. But a silent form
Was waiting in a corner. Up marble stairs,
He hurries from mirrored hall to hall, by glimmer
Of statues in niches. The Watcher stares,
        Red tabs upon his uniform.

Again he mounts the steps, alone,
Self-followed from mirrors to hall, the crowd
Of visitors waltzing below,
And looking from the bannisters
Upon the billiard tables, playerless,
Green-shaded, saw the Watcher with a frown
Behind a pillar, standing motionless
    Casting the shadow of a policeman.

Once, wandering from a hollow of asphodel,
Still flowering at mid-night, he saw the glint of
Gigantic row of columns beyond the dell,
    Templed, conical, unbedecked
And knew they were the holy ictyphalli
Curled hair for bushwood, bark or skin
Heavily veined. He worshipped, a tiny satyr,
    Mere prick beneath those vast erections.

Joyously through a gateway, came a running
Of little Jewish boys, their faces pale
As ivory or jasmine, from Lebanon
    To Eden. Garlanded, caressing,
Little girls ran with skip and leap. They hurried,
Moon-pointing, beyond the gate. They passed a pale
Of sacred laurel, flowers of the future. Love
    Fathered him with their happiness.

Always in terror of Olympic doom,
He climbed, despite his will, the spiral steps
Outside a building to a cobwebbed top-room.
    There bric-a-brac was in a jumble,
His forehead was distending, ears were drumming
As in the gastric fever of his childhood.
Despite his will, he climbed the steps, stumbling
    Where Mnemosyne lay in dust.

Dreaming, as sunlight idled, Maurice believed
He darted by with sticks of gelignite,
Unbarracked County Limerick, relieved
    His fellows, fought to the last bullet.
Daring Republican of hillside farm-yards,
Leader of raiding parties, digging at night,
He blew up lorries, captured British arms.
    Rain-hid, he cycled to Belmullet.

Drowsily Maurice was aware
Of someone by his bed. A melancholy
Man, sallow, with black moustache, sat there.
   'Where am I?' Voice was hollow.
The other brooded: 'Think.' His gaze
Was so reproachful, what was his guilt?
Could it be parricide? The stranger
   Still murmured: 'Think... Think.'

VI
One night he heard heart-breaking sound.
It was a sigh unworlding its sorrow.
Another followed. Slowly he counted
Four different sighs, one after another.
'My mother,' he anguished, 'and my sisters
Have passed away. I am alone, now,
Lost in myself in a mysterious
Darkness, the victim in a story.'
Far whistle of a train, the voice of steam.
Evil was peering through the peep-hole.

Suddenly heart began to beat
Too quickly, too loudly. It clamoured
As if it were stopping. He left the heat
And stumbled forward, hammered
The door, called out that he was dying.
Key turned. Body was picked up, carried
Beyond the ward, the bedwhite row
Of faces, into a private darkness.
Lock turned. He cried out. All was still.
He stood, limbs shivering in the chill.

He tumbled into half the truth:
Burial alive. His breath was shouting:
'Let, let me out.' But words were puny.
Fists hushed on a wall of inward-outness.
Knees crept along a floor that stirred
As softly. All was the same chill.
He knew the wall was circular
And air was catchcry in the stillness
For reason had returned to tell him
That he was in a padded cell.

The key had turned again. Blankets
Were flung into blackness as if to mock
The cringer on the floor. He wrapped
The bedclothes around his limbs, shocked back
To sanity. Lo! in memory yet,
Margaret came in a frail night-dress,
Feet bare, her heavy plaits let down
Between her knees, his pale protectress.
Nightly restraint, unwanted semen
Had ended their romantic dream.

Early next morning, he awakened,
Saw only greyness shining down
From a skylight on the grey walls
Of leather, knew, in anguish, his bowels
Had opened. He turned, shivering, all shent.
Wrapping himself in the filthied blankets,
Fearful of dire punishment,
He waited there until a blankness
Enveloped him... When he raised his head up,
Noon-light was gentle in the bedroom.

XVII
Summer was sauntering by,
Beyond the city spires,
As Maurice went a-walking
With Mr. Rhys by white-and-
Blue trams and jaunting cars,
Into a Picture Postcard
Of the Phoenix Park,
Along the People's Garden,
The railed-in chestnut trees,
Borders of marigold,
Clarkia and rose-beds,
Sunflower, blow-as-you-please.
The Wellington Monument:
Iron reliefs, old gunnage —
He wondered what they meant —
The Fifteen Acres, the Dog Pond.
But there was nothing beyond,
Only the Other Side.
His family lived there.
Thinking of them, he sighed.
As they turned back, he stared
Into the camera
Of mind, the double lens

Was darker. *Mensa*
Mensae. The passers-by
Kept off forbidden grass,
Stopped at the gay kiosk
For real Picture Postcards.
Slowly he counted the lamp-posts
And all the city spires,
Counted the blue-and-white
Trams and the outside cars.
He saw Columba O'Carroll
Who smiled as he raised his hat
Behind invisible bars,
Soon recognised the barracks,
The plane-trees, cannon balls,
Remembered aniseed balls
And Peggy's Leg, luck-bag.
A small boy must not lag.
They crossed over Kingsbridge.
The Guinness tugs were roped
Along their quay, cabs ranked
Outside the Railway Station:
Coupling of carriages.
A gig went spanking by.
He heard an engine whistle,
Piffle away in the distance.
Poetic Personification:
Hope frowned. Up Steeven's Lane,
He walked into his darkness.
Classical rustle of Harpies,
Their ordure at Swift's Gate.

XVIII
Rememorised, Maurice Devane
Went out, his future in every vein,
The Gate had opened. Down Steeven's Lane
The high wall of the Garden, to right
Of him, the Fountain with a horse-trough,
Illusions had become a story.
There was the departmental storey
Of Guinness's, God-given right
Of goodness in every barrel, tun,
They averaged. Upon that site

Of shares and dividends in sight
Of Watling Street and the Cornmarket,
At Number One in Thomas Street
Shone in the days of the ballad-sheet,
The house in which his mother was born.

A SERMON ON SWIFT
Friday, 11.30 a.m. April 28th, 1967

Gentle of hand, the Dean of St. Patrick's guided
My silence up the steps of the pulpit, put around
My neck the lesser microphone.
                                          'I feel
That you are blessing me, Mr. Dean.'
                                          Murmur
Was smile.

           In this first lay sermon, must I
Not speak the truth? Known scholars, specialists,
From far and near, were celebrating the third
Centenary of our great satirist.
They spoke of the churchman who kept his solemn gown,
Full-bottom, for Sunday and the Evening Lesson,
But hid from lectern the chuckling rhymster who went,
Bald-headed, into the night when modesty
Wantoned with beau and belle, his pen in hand.
Dull morning clapped his oldest wig on. He looked from
The Deanery window, spied the washerwomen
Bundling along, the hay carts swaying from
The Coombe, dropping their country smells, the hackney —
Clatter on cobbles — ready to share a quip
Or rebus with Sheridan and Tom Delaney,
Read an unfinished chapter to Vanessa
Or Stella, then rid his mind of plaguey curling —
Tongs, farthingales and fal-de-lals. A pox on
Night-hours when wainscot, walls, were dizziness,
Tympana, maddened by inner terror, celled
A man who did not know himself from Cain.
A Tale of a Tub, Gulliver's Travels, fables
And scatological poems, I pennied them on
The Quays, in second-hand book-stalls, when I was young,

Soon learned that humour, unlike the wit o' the Coffee
House, the Club, lengthens the features, smile hid by
A frown.
      Scarce had I uttered the words,
                                 'Dear Friends,
Dear Swiftians'—
                     when from the eastern window
The pure clear ray that Swift had known, entered the
Shady church and touched my brow. So blessed

Again, I gathered 'em up, four-letter words,
Street-cries, from the Liberties.
                          Ascend,
Our Lady of Filth, Cloacina, soiled goddess
Of paven sewers. Let Roman fountains, a-spray
With themselves, scatter again the imperious gift
Of self-in-sight.
                Celia on a close-stool
Stirs, ready to relace her ribs. Corinna,
Taking herself to pieces at midnight, slips from
The bed at noon, putting together soilures
And soft sores. Strephon half rouses from a dream
Of the flooding Tiber on his marriage-night,
When Chloe stoops out unable to contain her
Twelve cups of tea. Women are unsweet at times,
No doubt, yet how can willynilly resist
The pleasures of defaulting flesh?
                     My Sermon
Waits in the plethora of Rabelais, since
March veered with the rusty vane of Faith. I had reached
The House of Aries. Soon in the pure ray,
I am aware of my ancestor, Archbishop
Browne, hastily come from Christ Church, to dispel
Error and Popish superstition. He supped
Last night with Bishop Bale of Ossory,
Robustious as his plays, and, over the talk
And malmsey, forgot the confiscated wealth
Of abbeys.
             In prose, plain as pike, pillory,
In octosyllabic verse turning the two-way
Corner of rhyme, Swift wrote of privy matters
That have to be my text. The Lilliputian
March-by of the crack regiments saluting

On high the double pendulosity
Of Gulliver, glimpsed through a rent in his breeches;
The city square in admiration below. But who
Could blame the Queen when that almighty
Man hosed the private apartments of her palace,
Hissed down the flames of carelessness, leaving
The royal stables unfit for Houyhnhnms, or tell (in
A coarse aside) what the gigantic maidens
Of Brobdignab did in their playfulness with
The tiny Lemuel when they put him astride
A pap, broader than the mizzen mast of his
Wrecked ship, or hid him in the tangle below?
Reasonable century of Bolingbroke,
Hume, hundred-quilled Voltaire. Satyr and nymph
Disported in the bosk, prim avenues
Let in the classical sky. The ancient temples
Had been restored. Sculptures replaced the painted
Images of the saints. Altars were fuming,
And every capital was amaranthed.
Abstraction ruled the decumana of verse,
Careful caesura kept the middle silence
No syllable dared to cross.
                              Swift gave his savings
To mumbling hand, to tatters. Bare kibes ran after
Hoof as he rode beside the Liffey to sup
At Celbridge, brood with Vanessa in a star-bloomed
Bower on Tory politics, forget
Queen Anne, stride from a coffee-house to Whitehall
And with his pamphlets furrow the battle-fields
Of Europe once more, tear up the blood-signed contracts
Of Marlborough, Victualler of Victories;
While in St. Patrick's Cathedral the candling clerk
Shifted the shadows from pillar to pillar, shuffling
His years along the aisles with iron key.
Last gift of an unwilling patriot, Swift willed
To us a mansion of forgetfulness. I lodged
There for a year until Erata led me
Beyond the high-walled garden of Memory,
The Fountain of Hope, to the rewarding Gate,
Reviled but no longer defiled by harpies. And there
In Thomas Street, nigh to the busy stalls
Divine Abstraction smiled.

                                        My hour, above
Myself, draws to an end. Satiric rhymes
Are safe in the Deanery. So, I must find
A moral, search among my wits.
                                        I have
It.
   In his sudden poem *The Day of Judgment*
Swift borrowed the allegoric bolt of Jove,
Damned and forgave the human race, dismissed
The jest of life. Here is his secret belief
For sure: the doctrine of Erigena,
Scribing his way from West to East, from bang
Of monastery door, click o' the latch,
His sandals worn out, unsoled, a voice proclaiming
The World's mad business — Eternal Absolution.

PATRICK KAVANAGH
(1905-1967)

INNISKEEN ROAD: JULY EVENING

The bicycles go by in twos and threes—
There's a dance in Billy Brennan's barn to-night,
And there's the half-talk code of mysteries
And the wink-and-elbow language of delight.
Half-past eight and there is not a spot
Upon a mile of road, no shadow thrown
That might turn out a man or woman, not
A footfall tapping secrecies of stone.

I have what every poet hates in spite
Of all the solemn talk of contemplation.
Oh, Alexander Selkirk knew the plight
Of being king and government and nation.
A road, a mile of kingdom, I am king
Of banks and stones and every blooming thing.

THE GREAT HUNGER

I

Clay is the word and clay is the flesh
Where the potato-gatherers like mechanised scarecrows move
Along the side-fall of the hill — Maguire and his men.
If we watch them an hour is there anything we can prove
Of life as it is broken-backed over the Book
Of Death? Here crows gabble over worms and frogs
And the gulls like old newspapers are blown clear of the hedges,
     luckily.
Is there some light of imagination in these wet clods?
Or why do we stand here shivering?
                              Which of these men
Loved the light and the queen
Too long virgin? Yesterday was summer. Who was it promised
     marriage to himself
Before apples were hung from the ceilings for Hallowe'en?
We will wait and watch the tragedy to the last curtain,
Till the last soul passively like a bag of wet clay
Rolls down the side of the hill, diverted by the angles
Where the plough missed or a spade stands, straitening the way.

A dog lying on a torn jacket under a heeled-up cart,
A horse nosing along the posied headland, trailing
A rusty plough. Three heads hanging between wide-apart
Legs. October playing a symphony on a slack wire paling.
Maguire watches the drills flattened out
And the flints that lit a candle for him on a June altar
Flameless. The drills slipped by and the days slipped by
And he trembled his head away and ran free from the world's
      halter,
And thought himself wiser than any man in the townland
When he laughed over pints of porter
Of how he came free from every net spread
In the gaps of experience. He shook a knowing head
And pretended to his soul
That children are tedious in hurrying fields of April
Where men are spanging across wide furrows.
Lost in the passion that never needs a wife —
The pricks that pricked were the pointed pins of harrows.
Children scream so loud that the crows could bring
The seed of an acre away with crow-rude jeers.
Patrick Maguire, he called his dog and he flung a stone in the air
And hallooed the birds away that were the birds of the years.

Turn over the weedy clods and tease out the tangled skeins.
What is he looking for there?
He thinks it is a potato, but we know better
Than his mud-gloved fingers probe in this insensitive hair.

'Move forward the basket and balance it steady
In this hollow. Pull down the shafts of that cart, Joe,
And straddle the horse,' Maguire calls.
'The wind's over Brannagan's, now that means rain.
Graip up some withered stalks and see that no potato falls
Over the tail-board going down the ruckety pass —
And that's a job we'll have to do in December,
Gravel it and build a kerb on the bog-side. Is that Cassidy's ass
Out in my clover? Curse o' God —
Where is that dog?
Never where he's wanted.' Maguire grunts and spits
Through a clay-wattled moustache and stares about him from
      the height.
His dream changes again like the cloud-swung wind
And he is not so sure now if his mother was right
When she praised the man who made a field his bride.

Watch him, watch him, that man on a hill whose spirit
Is a wet sack flapping about the knees of time.
He lives that his little fields may stay fertile when his own body
Is spread in the bottom of a ditch under two coulters crossed
    in Christ's Name.

He was suspicious in his youth as a rat near strange bread,
When girls laughed; when they screamed he knew that meant
The cry of fillies in season. He could not walk
The easy road to his destiny. He dreamt
The innocence of young brambles to hooked treachery.
O the grip, O the grip of irregular fields! No man escapes.
It could not be that back of the hills love was free
And ditches straight.
No monster hand lifted up children and put down apes
As here.
                   'O God if I had been wiser!'
That was his sigh like the brown breeze in the thistles.
He looks towards his house and haggard. 'O God if I had been
    wiser!'
But now a crumpled leaf from the whitethorn bushes
Darts like a frightened robin, and the fence
Shows the green of after-grass through a little window,
And he knows that his own heart is calling his mother a liar.
God's truth is life — even the grotesque shapes of its foulest fire.

The horse lifts its head and cranes
Through the whins and stones
To lip late passion in the crawling clover.
In the gap there's a bush weighted with boulders like morality,
The fools of life bleed if they climb over.

The wind leans from Brady's, and the coltsfoot leaves are holed
    with rust,
Rain fills the cart-tracks and the sole-plate grooves;
A yellow sun reflects in Donaghmoyne
The poignant light in puddles shaped by hooves.
Come with me, Imagination, into this iron house
And we will watch from the doorway the years run back,
And we will know what a peasant's left hand wrote on the page.
Be easy, October. No cackle hen, horse neigh, tree sough, duck
    quack.

III

Poor Paddy Maguire, a fourteen-hour day
He worked for years. It was he that lit the fire
And boiled the kettle and gave the cows their hay.
His mother tall hard as a Protestant spire
Came down the stairs barefoot at the kettle-call
And talked to her son sharply: 'Did you let'
The hens out, you?' She had a venomous drawl
And a wizened face like moth-eaten leatherette.
Two black cats peeped between the banisters
And gloated over the bacon-fizzling pan.
Outside the window showed tin canisters.
The snipe of Dawn fell like a whirring stone
And Patrick on a headland stood alone.

The pull is on the traces, it is March
And a cold old black wind is blowing from Dundalk.
The twisting sod rolls over on her back —
The virgin screams before the irresistible sock.
No worry on Maguire's mind this day
Except that he forgot to bring his matches.
'Hop back there Polly, hoy back, woa, wae,'
From every second hill a neighbour watches
With all the sharpened interest of rivalry.
Yet sometimes when the sun comes through a gap
These men know God the Father in a tree:
The Holy Spirit is the rising sap,
And Christ will be the green leaves that will come
At Easter from the sealed and guarded tomb.

Primroses and the unearthly start of ferns
Among the blackthorn shadows in the ditch,
A dead sparrow and an old waistcoat. Maguire learns
As the horses turn slowly round the which is which
Of love and fear and things half born to mind.
He stands between the plough-handles and he sees
At the end of a long furrow his name signed
Among the poets, prostitute's. With all miseries
He is one. Here with the unfortunate
Who for half-moments of paradise
Pay out good days and wait and wait
For sunlight-woven cloaks. O to be wise
As Respectability that knows the price of all things
And marks God's truth in pounds and pence and farthings.

IV
April, and no one able to calculate
How far is it to harvest. They put down
The seeds blindly with sensuous groping fingers,
And sensual sleep dreams subtly underground.
Tomorrow is Wednesday — who cares?
'Remember Eileen Farrelly? I was thinking
A man might do a damned sight worse...' That voice
    is blown
Through a hole in a garden wall —
And who was Eileen now cannot be known.

The cattle are out on grass,
The corn is coming up evenly.
The farm folk are hurrying to catch Mass:
Christ will meet them at the end of the world, the slow and
    speedier.
But the fields say: only Time can bless.

Maguire knelt beside a pillar where he could spit
Without being seen. He turned an old prayer round:
'Jesus, Mary and Joseph pray for us
Now and at the Hour.' Heaven dazzled death.
'Wonder should I cross-plough that turnip-ground.'
The tension broke. The congregation lifted its head
As one man and coughed in unison.
Five hundred hearts were hungry for life —
Who lives in Christ shall never die the death.
And the candle-lit Altar and the flowers
And the pregnant Tabernacle lifted a moment to Prophecy
Out of the clayey hours.
Maguire sprinkled his face with holy water
As the congregation stood up for the Last Gospel.
He rubbed the dust off his knees with his palm, and then
Coughed the prayer phlegm up from his throat and sighed:
        Amen.

Once one day in June when he was walking
Among his cattle in the Yellow Meadow
He met a girl carrying a basket —
And he was then a young and heated fellow.
Too earnest, too earnest! He rushed beyond the thing
To the unreal. And he saw Sin
Written in letters larger than John Bunyan dreamt of.

For the strangled impulse there is no redemption.
And that girl was gone and he was counting
The dangers in the fields where love ranted
He was helpless. He saw his cattle
And stroked their flanks in lieu of wife to handle.
He would have changed the circle if he could,
The circle that was the grass track where he ran.
Twenty times a day he ran round the field
And still there was no winning-post where the runner is cheered
    home.
Desperately he broke the tune,
But however he tried always the same melody crept up from the
    background,
The dragging step of a ploughman going home through the
    guttery
Headlands under an April-watery moon.
Religion, the fields and the fear of the Lord
And Ignorance giving him the coward's blow,
He dare not rise to pluck the fantasies
From the fruited Tree of Life. He bowed his head
And saw a wet weed twined about his toe.

VI

Health and wealth and love he too dreamed of in May
As he sat on the railway slope and watched the children of
    the place
Picking up a primrose here and a daisy there —
They were picking up life's truth singly. But he dreamt
    of the Absolute envased bouquet —

All or nothing.   And it was nothing.   For God is not all
In one place, complete
Till Hope comes in and takes it on his shoulder —
O Christ, that is what you have done for us:
In a crumb of bread the whole mystery is.

He read the symbol too sharply and turned
From the five simple doors of sense
To the door whose combination lock has puzzled
Philosopher and priest and common dunce.

Men build their heavens as they build their circles
Of friends. God is in the bits and pieces of Everyday —
A kiss here and a laugh again, and sometimes tears,
A pearl necklace round the neck of poverty.

He sat on the railway slope and watched the evening,
Too beautifully perfect to use,
And his three wishes were three stones too sharp to sit on,
Too hard to carve. Three frozen idols of a speechless muse.

From TARRY FLYNN

On an apple-ripe September morning
Through the mist-chill fields I went
With a pitch-fork on my shoulder
Less for use than for devilment.

The threshing mill was set-up, I knew,
In Cassidy's haggard last night,
And we owed them a day at the threshing
Since last year. O it was delight

To be paying bills of laughter
And chaffy gossip in kind
With work thrown in to ballast
The fantasy-soaring mind.

As I crossed the wooden bridge I wondered
As I looked into the drain
If ever a summer morning should find me
Shovelling up eels again.

And I thought of the wasps' nest in the bank
And how I got chased one day
Leaving the drag and the scraw-knife behind,
How I covered my face with hay.

The wet leaves of the cocksfoot
Polished my boots as I
Went round by the glistening bog-holes
Lost in unthinking joy.

I'll be carrying bags to-day, I mused,
The best job at the mill
With plenty of time to talk of our loves
As we wait for the bags to fill.

Maybe Mary might call round...
And then I came to the haggard gate,
And I knew as I entered that I had come
Through fields that were part of no earthly estate.

SHANCODUFF

My black hills have never seen the sun rising,
Eternally they look north towards Armagh.
Lot's wife would not be salt if she had been
Incurious as my black hills that are happy
When dawn whitens Glassdrummond chapel.

My hills hoard the bright shillings of March
While the sun searches in every pocket.
They are my Alps and I have climbed the Matterhorn
With a sheaf of hay for three perishing calves
In the field under the Big Forth of Rocksavage.

The sleety winds fondle the rushy beards of Shancoduff
While the cattle-drovers sheltering in the Featherna Bush
Look up and say: 'Who owns them hungry hills
That the water-hen and snipe must have forsaken?
A poet? Then by heavens he must be poor'
I hear and is my heart not badly shaken?

Monaghan 1934

THE LONG GARDEN

It was the garden of the golden apples,
A long garden between a railway and a road,
In the sow's rooting where the hen scratches
We dipped our fingers in the pockets of God.

In the thistly hedge old boots were flying sandals
By which we travelled through the childhood skies,
Old buckets rusty-holed with half-hung handles
Were drums to play when old men married wives.

The pole that lifted the clothes-line in the middle
Was the flag-pole on a prince's palace when
We looked at it though fingers crossed to riddle
In evening sunlight miracles for men.

It was the garden of the golden apples,
And when the Carrick train went by we knew
That we could never die till something happened
Like wishing for a fruit that never grew,

Or wanting to be up on Candle-Fort
Above the village with its shops and mill.
The racing cyclists' gasp-gapped reports
Hinted of pubs where life can drink his fill.

And when the sun went down into Drumcatton
And the New Moon by its little finger swung
From the telegraph wires, we knew how God had happened
And what the blackbird in the whitethorn sang.

It was the garden of the golden apples,
The half-way house where we had stopped a day
Before we took the west road to Drumcatton
Where the sun was always setting on the play.

BLUEBELLS FOR LOVE

There will be bluebells growing under the big trees
And you will be there and I will be there in May;
For some other reason we both will have to delay
The evening in Dunshaughlin — to please
Some imagined relation,
So both of us came to walk through that plantation.

We will be interested in the grass,
In an old bucket-hoop, in the ivy that weaves
Green incongruity among dead leaves,
We will put on surprise at carts that pass —
Only sometimes looking sideways at the bluebells in the plantation
And never frighten them with too wild an exclamation.

We will be wise, we will not let them guess
That we are watching them or they will pose
A mere façade like boys
Caught out in virtue's naturalness.
We will not impose on the bluebells in that plantation
Too much of our desire's adulation.

We will have other loves — or so they'll think;
The primroses or the ferns or the briars,
Or even the rusty paling wires,
Or the violets on the sunless sorrel bank,
Only as an aside the bluebells in the plantation
Will mean a thing to our dark contemplation.

We'll know love little by little, glance by glance.
Ah, the clay under these roots is so brown!
We'll steal from Heaven while God is in the town —
I caught an angel smiling in a chance
Look through the tree-trunks of the plantation
As you and I walked slowly to the station.

A CHRISTMAS CHILDHOOD

I
One side of the potato-pits was white with frost —
How wonderful that was, how wonderful!
And when we put our ears to the paling-post
The music that came out was magical.

The light between the ricks of hay and straw
Was a hole in Heaven's gable. An apple tree
With its December-glinting fruit we saw —
O you, Eve, were the world that tempted me

To eat the knowledge that grew in clay
And death the germ within it! Now and then
I can remember something of the gay
Garden that was childhood's. Again

The tracks of cattle to a drinking-place,
A green stone lying sideways in a ditch
Or any common sight the transfigured face
Of a beauty that the world did not touch.

II
My father played the melodion
Outside at our gate;
There were stars in the morning east
And they danced to his music.

Across the wild bogs his melodion called
To Lennons and Callans.
As I pulled on my trousers in a hurry
I knew some strange thing had happened.

Outside in the cow-house my mother
Made the music of milking;
The light of her stable-lamp was a star
And the frost of Bethlehem made it twinkle.

A water-hen screeched in the bog,
Mass-going feet
Crunched the wafer-ice on the pot-holes,
Somebody wistfully twisted the bellows wheel.

My child poet picked out the letters
On the grey stone,
In silver the wonder of a Christmas townland,
The winking glitter of a frosty dawn.

Cassiopeia was over
Cassidy's hanging hill,
I looked and three whin bushes rode across
The horizon – the Three Wise Kings.

An old man passing said:
'Can't he make it talk' –
The melodion. I hid in the doorway
And tightened the belt of my box-pleated coat.

I nicked six nicks on the door-post
With my penknife's big blade –
There was a little one for cutting tobacco.
And I was six Christmases of age.

My father played the melodion,
My mother milked the cows,
And I had a prayer like a white rose pinned
On the Virgin Mary's blouse.

SPRAYING THE POTATOES

The barrels of blue potato-spray
Stood on a headland of July
Beside an orchard wall where roses
Were young girls hanging from the sky.

The flocks of green potato-stalks
Were blossoms spread for sudden flight,
The Kerr's Pinks in a frivelled blue,
The Arran Banners wearing white.

And over that potato-field
A lazy veil of woven sun.
Dandelions growing on headlands, showing
Their unloved hearts to everyone.

And I was there with the knapsack sprayer
On the barrel's edge poised. A wasp was floating
Dead on a sunken briar leaf
Over a copper-poisoned ocean.

The axle-roll of a rut-locked cart
Broke the burnt stick of noon in two.
An old man came through a corn-field
Remembering his youth and some Ruth he knew.

He turned my way. 'God further the work.'
He echoed an ancient farming prayer.
I thanked him. He eyed the potato-drills.
He said: 'You are bound to have good ones there.'

We talked and our talk was a theme of kings,
A theme for strings. He hunkered down
In the shade of the orchard wall. O roses
The old man dies in the young girl's frown.

And poet lost to potato fields,
Remembering the lime and copper smell
Of the spraying barrels he is not lost
Or till blossomed stalks cannot weave a spell.

EPIC

I have lived in important places, times
When great events were decided, who owned
That half a rood of rock, a no-man's land
Surrounded by our pitchfork-armed claims.
I heard the Duffys shouting 'Damn your soul'
And old McCabe stripped to the waist, seen
Step the plot defying blue cast-steel –
'Here is the march along these iron stones'
That was the year of the Munich bother. Which
Was more important? I inclined
To lose my faith in Ballyrush and Gortin
Till Homer's ghost came whispering to my mind
He said: I made the Iliad from such
A local row. Gods make their own importance.

IF EVER YOU GO TO DUBLIN TOWN

If ever you go to Dublin town
In a hundred years or so
Inquire for me in Baggot Street
And what I was like to know.
O he was a queer one,
Fol dol the di do,
He was a queer one
I tell you.

My great-grandmother knew him well,
He asked her to come and call
On him in his flat and she giggled at the thought
Of a young girl's lovely fall.
O he was dangerous,
Fol dol the di do,
He was dangerous
I tell you.

On Pembroke Road look out for my ghost,
Dishevelled with shoes untied,
Playing through the railings with little children
Whose children have long since died.
O he was a nice man,
Fol dol the di do,
He was a nice man
I tell you.

Go into a pub and listen well
If my voice still echoes there,
Ask the men what their grandsires thought
And tell them to answer fair.
O he was eccentric,
Fol dol the di do,
He was eccentric
I tell you.

He had the knack of making men feel
As small as they really were
Which meant as great as God had made them
But as males they disliked his air.
O he was a proud one,
Fol dol the di do,
He was a proud one
I tell you.

If ever you go to Dublin town
In a hundred years or so
Sniff for my personality,
Is it Vanity's vapour now?
O he was a vain one,
Fol dol the di do,
He was a vain one
I tell you.

I saw his name with a hundred others
In a book in the library,
It said he had never fully achieved
His potentiality.
O he was slothful,
Fol dol the di do,
He was slothful
I tell you.

He knew that posterity has no use
For anything but the soul,
The lines that speak the passionate heart,
The spirit that lives alone.
O he was a lone one,
Fol dol the di do
Yet he lived happily
I tell you.

PRELUDE

Give us another poem, he said
Or they will think your muse is dead;
Another middle-age departure
Of Apollo from the trade of archer.
Bring out a book as soon as you can
To let them see you're a living man,
Whose comic spirit is untamed
Though sadness for a little claimed
The precedence; and tentative
You pulled your punch and wondered if
Old Cunning Silence might not be
A better bet than poetry.

You have not got the countenance
To hold the angle of pretence,
That angry bitter look for one
Who knows that art's a kind of fun;
That all true poems laugh inwardly
Out of grief-born intensity.
Dullness alone can get you beat
And so can humour's counterfeit.
You have not got a chance with fraud
And might as well be true to God.

Then link your laughter out of doors
In sunlight past the sick-faced whores
Who chant the praise of love that isn't
And bring their bastards to be Christened
At phoney founts by bogus priests
With rites mugged up by journalists
Walk past professors looking serious

Fondling an unpublished thesis –
'A child! my child! my darling son'
Some Poets of Nineteen Hundred and One.

Note well the face profoundly grave,
An empty mind can house a knave.
Be careful to show no defiance,
They've made pretence into a science;
Card-sharpers of the art committee
Working all the provincial cities,
They cry 'Eccentric' if they hear
A voice that seems at all sincere.
Fold up their table and their gear
And with the money disappear.

But satire is unfruitful prayer,
Only wild shoots of pity there,
And you must go inland and be
Lost in compassion's ecstasy,
Where suffering soars in summer air –
The millstone has become a star.

Count then your blessings, hold in mind
All that has loved you or been kind:
Those women on their mercy missions,
Rescue work with kiss or kitchens,
Perceiving through the comic veil
The poet's spirit in travail.
Gather the bits of road that were
Not gravel to the traveller
But eternal lanes of joy
On which no man who walks can die.
Bring in the particular trees
That caught you in their mysteries,
And love again the weeds that grew
Somewhere specially for you.
Collect the river and the stream
That flashed upon a pensive theme,
And a positive world make,
A world man's world cannot shake.
And do not lose love's resolution
Though face to face with destitution.

If Platitude should claim a place
Do not denounce his humble face;
His sentiments are well intentioned
He has a part in the larger legend.

So now my gentle tiger burning
In the forest of no-yearning
Walk on serenely, do not mind
That Promised Land you thought to find,
Where the worldly-wise and rich take over
The mundane problems of the lower,
Ignore Power's schismatic sect,
Lovers alone lovers protect.

CANAL BANK WALK

Leafy-with-love banks and the green waters of the canal
Pouring redemption for me, that I do
The will of God, wallow in the habitual, the banal,
Grow with nature again as before I grew.
The bright stick trapped, the breeze adding a third
Party to the couple kissing on an old seat,
And a bird gathering materials for the nest for the Word
Eloquently new and abandoned to its delirious beat.
O unworn world enrapture me, encapture me in a web
Of fabulous grass and eternal voices by a beech,
Feed the gaping need of my senses, give me ad lib
To pray unselfconsciously with overflowing speech
For this soul needs to be honoured with a new dress woven
From green and blue things and arguments that cannot be
    proven.

LINES WRITTEN ON A SEAT
ON THE GRAND CANAL, DUBLIN
'Erected to the Memory of Mrs. Dermot O'Brien'

*epitaph for
Kavanagh too —*

O commemorate me where there is water,
Canal water preferably, so stilly
Greeny at the heart of summer. Brother
Commemorate me thus beautifully.
Where by a lock niagarously roars
The falls for those who sit in the tremendous silence
Of mid-July. No one will speak in prose
Who finds his way to these Parnassian islands.
A swan goes by head low with many apologies,
Fantastic light looks through the eyes of bridges –
And look! a barge comes bringing from Athy
And other far-flung towns mythologies.
O commemorate me with no hero-courageous
Tomb – just a canal-bank seat for the passer-by.

DENIS DEVLIN
(1908-1959)

MEMOIRS OF A TURCOMAN DIPLOMAT

OTELI ASIA PALAS, INC.

Evenings ever more willing lapse into my world's evening,
Birds, like Imperial emblems, in their thin, abstract singing,
Announce some lofty Majesty whose embassies are not
     understood,
Thrushes' and finches' chords, like the yellow and blue skies
     changing place,
I hold my stick, old-world, the waiters know me,
And sip at my European drink, while sunlight falls,
Like thick Italian silks over the square houses into the
     Bosphorus
Ladies, I call you women now, from out my emptied
     tenderness,
All dead in the wars, before and after war,
I toast you my adventures with your beauty!
Where the domes of Sinan shiver like ductile violets in the
     rain of light.

To the Franks, I suppose it's ugly, this brick and oblong,
When a rare sunlight, rare birdsong,
Compose the absolute kingdom far in the sky
The Franks must ask how it was known, how reached,
     how governed, how let die?
This woman who passes by, sideways, by your side:
There was one you loved for years and years;
Suddenly the jaw is ugly, the shoulders fall,
Provoking but resentment, hardly tears.

THE GOLDEN HORN

We all have a magic kingdom, some have two,
And cry: 'O my city on the Golden Horn, and
     O my you!'
Discover, in the bee flaunting his black and gold among the
     foliage in the frieze,
You are not what you thought, you are someone like all
     these,
The most ardent young man turn, at the drop of a black hat,
Into some rabbity sort of clerk, some heart-affairs diplomat,

A John of the Cross into a Curia priest.
It was years ago. It is not now like when the century
        began—
Though apple and peach lie brilliant on the dark,
And mineral worlds on the dark sky shine,
And the red mouth breathes in; thine is mine,
And the careless Atlantic inhales the Thames, the Tagus
        and the Seine,
Murmuring back and murmuring forward beasts and sonata
        scores and Ophelian rags —
Where a girl in her balldress was a light on the wave,
Where a dying flare was like a firefly on the wave,
Where all the waves shivered with phosphorous under the
        moon's glacial withdrawal —
'Me voici ignorant' : so a poet my father read.
The Empire born again, old pendants will rake up the dead.

My father thought my feeling could take fire by the vibrant
        Seine
And a tough intellect he constructed in Gottingen,
He thought, the citadels of Anatolia I could justify
Making what's hungry full, what's ragged spry.
Opalescent on the unbloodied green, the Sultan's battle
        horse,
The hungry cavalry, rearing and screaming in the mist:
We put them down, these Franks, in their sweaty leather
        and blasphemous curse,
Our salaried Levantine admirals sank their trading ships.
It happened: the Prophet conquered with murder in his
        hand and honour in his crescent lips.

Put it down to a thick heart and a thick pate,
Such puritanic temperament's outgrown:
Now some international Secretary-General throws a lump of bait
And laughs and says my country's not my own.

There was a professor who said: 'The horse must go!'
And certain poets praised him to their shame,
Except in County Cork and Mexico
And where the quick darlings to us from the Cossacks came.
In the Foreign Office, they humorously ask my advice,
My father had money, I was posted from place to place:
What can I tell them? even if I got it right?

There would be protocol about the right time and the
right place,
And even not too sentimental about the corps of horse
Dancing between the up-country captains' harsh knees
They could assert that horses than humanity were worse —

And that our Westernising dictator, though free was no
    longer free
When at Smyrne he tumbled the chatterbox Greeks into
    the sea,
Turk lieutenants, waxed moustashes and all, and spiritless
    mugs of tea.

WARS OF RELIGION
All is when I remember and forget
The Prophet drops the sword and shuts the Book
Down the green wind the Lord came, I met
The Lord, but did not feel or hear or look,

Interrupted by the Exarch shouting, we robbed Greece—
It's true — those comedians with their epics,
Their Aphrodite, their Achilles, their Golden Fleece,
Shouting the Prophet down, with their rational septics,

Even their best, their Hector, did not know,
Or mother Venus with her bog and milk,
Gesso Olympians dancing heel and toe —
Why should a Turk care about that ilk?

FOUR TURKISH WOMEN
The true, the loyal moon, not like her mother,
She was the plasma we assembled to:
All sky flows, water and blood and spittle,
Mother degraded in her human brew.

Moon! rest our emblem... not like Europeans
Whose stupid sun discovers all their dirt.
O Crescent, sweet and careless above the water —
Yet infidel fingers hurt

A woman, my Frankish Friend's one wife,
In a far Latin villa held his hand;
It was night all at once, and kind of grief
And kind of laughter, and kind with hand in hand.

ANATOLIA
In the high country, there is no food for ghosts,
The dead stay underground, which is their place
We had enough to do to keep the Arabs and the Bulgars
        in their place
If the dead have bad dreams they live in us, querulous
        and lost.

Must we believe that hatred or freedom, the Sultan Ahmet
        risen on his medieval horse, turns to love?
Fail to regret the Empire, the Franks and the Hohenstaufen?
Europa and the Turk Bull?
The President of the Republic bends this way and that,
A bubble on the corner of his lips,
The Franks have their shopkeeper saints, Saint Thomas
        Aquinas,
(And Saint Thomas putting his hand in the Wound)
How can you think it's sure if you're a coward?

RISTORANT PIKNIK
The trams go tired home in the Istliqal Caddesi,
Rue du Pera, we said — the Frankish end.
The waiter flicks off a crumb. It was lamb and rice;
Would you raise your knife to stick an indifferent friend?

THE TURKISH FOR GREEK IS ROMAN
Why we call the Greeks Romans I know not
Nor without grammar do I care not:
Both were here before we were, but hear not
Nor grudge, nor love nor hate, they're lost and know not.

THE WHITE CITY
The Sava and the Danube like two horses folded, mane
        on mane,
And there were dogs which lapped the water up:
Pale sunlight and pale water, as if some great poet
Said there was peace, like Goethe, and there was peace.

The sunlight pressing on the eyelids, on the waters;
Only ten years ago the invaders came,
The pretty guide talked on and showed our party —
In which were former Nazis, former Fascists —
Photo-posters of men hanging like blotting paper,
Dirty blood on dirty children, dirty mothers
The willowy waters of the Sava bathed;
Only three hundred years ago
Sulymein the Magnificent
Sick and sad outside Belgrade.

Who knows his expectations, free or slave?
Join me, Johannes, down this pretty brace:
One said, or could have sung, Come out with me,
The other, A truce to talk of genocide, and nation and race!

Tuck in your trews, Johannes, my boy, be led by me,
These girls are kind. And we're all the rage now,
        whisky-flushed men of our age,
The callow and the sallow and the fallow wiped off
        the page!

FAREWELL AND GOOD

She I loved so much will not appear again
Brilliant to my eyes as once she held me, nor
To inhuman eyes in an angel-foaming world.

What use my hermit grief to a world bitten in self,
Bland under omen, but to make more its useless griefs?
Why must, as absence ages, she the more instant cling?

Grief cannot doctor my birthday evil that diminished her
Nor be voucher for recompense of pain at heaven's gates
Nor by crying it for relief do I purge it. Nothing forgets:

Not wisdom teased from the wax and crumble of all flesh,
Powdering between thumb and finger: O wash in moon-milk!
Suck the drug simples in our rock-night scratched by man

In eruptions of mineral continents scruffling to settle down:
Nor though spring lust and shine on the sea and chaffinches
        chatter,
Though light from sunlight down to tombs give me my kind:

Whatever I do, unreal, I may find my hand, once hers,
Bled on the wall in a crack of anger and veins blocked
And eyes glazed that will break open to hers no more;

At any time of the day and night, struck by a wind-flash
In snood of leaves or in phantasms of sleep assembling her
        form,
I restore my kingdom in her, the real that deepened the
        dreamed-on

Ritual loves of legend women admired in childhood:
Then remembrance stings my reason, both entangled in
Grief which webs movement and is merely want.

Still the complaint still no comfort to her and me split
Like a glass, like life split by some Sistine hand,
Our life that brimmed over like diamonds in our light.

EVE IN MY LEGEND

The world turns round and leaves the sun.
City fathers, light her way!
Switch on the lights for her! It's done,
For her the town's a Milky Way.
I am near mindless, I could mime
The passions that consume Time.

Today we passed from a yellow street
Into a black one, high and cold
I said to her, I turned it neat,
   'Your hair's the sun now, warmth and gold.'
The too few suns whose earth, to thrive
Can but in Love's eyes come alive.

Once I had kissed her eyes and seen
My love there made whole by their rays
I knew her better than if we'd been
Together a hundred nights and days
And air whose sunny tongues are birds
Bore with ease our heavy words

As she from my drugged side took life.
I feel like Adam who in sleep
Gave birth to Eve, daughter and wife
Whence his far brood would sow and reap,
Half monster, half philosopher,
Movement by mood conceiving her.

And now stop for a mental spell
The forest-eyed, obsidian After!
Yet let that hundred-headed tell
My arms full of her blond laughter
Nothing to know that is not she
Nor she know anything but me.

ANK'HOR VAT

The antlered forests
Move down to the sea.
Here the dung-filled jungle pauses

Buddha has covered the walls of the great temple
With the vegetative speed of his imagery

Let us wait, hand in hand

No Western god or saint
Ever smiled with the lissome fury of this god
Who holds in doubt
The wooden stare of Apollo
Our Christian crown of thorns:

There is no mystery in the luminous lines
Of that high, animal face
The smile, sad, humouring and equal
Blesses without obliging
Loves without condescension;
The god, clear as spring-water
Sees through everything, while everything
Flows through him

A fling of flowers here
Whose names I do not know
Downy, scarlet gullets
Green legs yielding and closing

While, at my mental distance from passion,
The prolific divinity of the temple
Is a quiet lettering on vellum.

Let us lie down before him
His look will flow like oil over us.

THE COLOURS OF LOVE

to my wife Caren

Women that are loved are more than lovable
    Their beauty absolute blows:
But little, like the urgent, carnal soul,
    More than its leaves so mortal in the rose.

O rose! O more than red mortality!
    What can my love have said
That made me her imagine more than be?
    Her mind more than mind, blood more than red?

As the noise of cars and chariots fades,
    And the empire of the stars
Reconquers with its bright and lusty blades
    My room, and heals my scars,

I raise my arms to that mistress planet,
    Venus, whose hunting priests explain
My heart and the rush of legend on it,
    Making me man again!

Those beautiful women shone against the dark
With flowers upon the breast, and birds
Disturbed by foreknowledge, sang some notes.
There were unshed tears, reproach and fret;
I wondered if their women's time was yet.

And the flowers like milk in a dark pantry at night
Offered themselves to the groping hand:
The cliffs fell faster than tears
Reaching that pain'where feeling does not matter;
Nor through the house the ghosts' averse patter.

Repeating their old theme of the unknown
Birds or women never did translate:
It was as if eternity were breathing
Through the small breathing of the flowers
Shining upon its breast with speechless light.

Remember! do you think I could forget?
The pigeons growl like dogs in sleep remote.
Yet now if you should ask, I could not yet
Forswear that fascination, break that note

Which death in his lush garden exercised,
The habit of repentance feeds the sin,
I know that sloth the solitaries disguised,
I know the door the sweet fogs entered in.

As memory more fitful daylight makes,
Death can increase his holdings in my sleep:
While benched and cheery drunks pull up their stakes
For one more day in search of food and keep.

Abundant stone figures sun themselves
In the precarious granary of the light,
Husbanded by our father, our farmer, selves
Against subversive, supernatural blight.

Voices from the shrubbery nearby:
 'Smile with your eyes,' one says, 'what sweet invention!'
What did that Mediterranean nymph reply?
 'Smile with your fables and their sweet intention.'

Listen in the gold confusion of the wheat,
Inside mortality, to what can move you:
The protests, the protection, the defeat —
 'When I am gone,' the voice asks, 'who will
        love you?'

The crackling lightwaves overhead
Minimise our human year.
O blond haunches! O white bed!
O harmless, ultramundane fear!

Refuge of sinners! Night by night!
Bury your head beneath the sheet:
Still the unworldly angels fight
And casually tear their meat.

It cannot well be said of love and death
That love is better and that death is worse,
Unless we buy death off with loving breath
So he may rent his beauty with our purse.

But is that beauty, is that beauty death?
No, it's the mask by which we're drawn to him,
It is with our consent death finds his breath;
Love is death's beauty and annexes him.

While pestilence feathered down, the hero wasted
Nor would he 'cry aloud' or 'breathe a prayer'
It being essential to the gall he tasted
That bitterness only bitterness can share.

How could he climb the glen through ruined farms
Nor hear his dead fathers take up arms?
He is a hero, and must make his peace
With all that's left — a few unfrocked police!

I think of seal-barking seas in the West,
It's all between a cry and a caress,
Where the windy islands yield no yeast
And men bake their own bread of bitterness;

Carry the soil of salvation in their arms
Lay it on rock and put down the seed,
It's all in a bed that chills and warms
With too much brood and too little feed.

I saw him move among the iron leaves
Which were to carbonise through his love's breast.
Hers, and the graves of lechers, louts and thieves,
Would sag and musty change be all their rest.

When leaves have fallen and there's nothing left
But plainsong from ascetic bony birds,
I say a prayer for all who are bereft
Of love, of leafy summer, of loving words.

I met a kinsman in the market-place,
Singing, and as he sang my courage grew,
It was about betrayal and disgrace,
He said 'Love fails but love of love stays true' .

Singing in vain and formal in the shade
The noble poverty those houses made.

Divinities of my youth,
Expound to me my truth;

Whether from Judah or Rome
Or my nearer Gaeldom.

The driven horse formalises
His speed for prestige and for prizes,

The girl swinging on the swing
Of the convent, makes me sing

And apples drop like centuries from
The tree of life, so long in bloom;

But divinities of my youth,
You can no longer tell the truth,

It is too much a struggle to
Keep quality confined to you.

When Spring with her lambs and sea-cries rises,
Her fluent fantasy makes a mock of me;
I throw off my absolutist devices
And dissemble in the loose, resplendent sea:

Yet think on how San Juan, bitter and bare,
Wrapt in his drama, sent his cry above,
And though, through layer on suffocating layer
Nothing came back, he loved; and so I love.

At the Bar du Départ drink farewell
And say no word you'll be remembered by;
Nor Prince nor President can ever tell
Where love ends or when it does or why.

Down the boulevard the lights come forth
Like my rainflowers trembling all through Spring,
Blue and Yellow in the Celtic North ...
The stone's ripple weakens, ring by ring.

Better no love than love, which, through loving
Leads to no love. The ripples come to rest ...
Ah me! how all that young year I was moving
To take her dissolution to my breast!

FROM GOVERNMENT BUILDINGS

Evening lapses. No pity or pain, the badgered
Great get home, and the little, tomorrow's anchorage,
All smiling, sour the milk of charity,
Like the pyrrhonist poets, Love's saboteurs.

The clerks fan out and the lamps; and I look inwards:
What turns amuse you now? with whom, not me! do
You cower in Time, whose palsied pulse is nimbler
A hair's breadth when want and have are equal?

My room sighs empty with malignant waiting;
The November wind slows down outside, wheeling
Twig and awning on the brick balcony,
A wind with hackles up. In Rome at evening

Swallows traced eggshapes on the vellum sky,
The wind was warm with blue rain in Dublin;
When the culture-heroes explored the nether world
It was voiceless beasts on the move made Death terrible.

Friendship I will not, barring you; to have witness does:
Doll birds, dogs with their social nose, by day
Are touchstone. But at night my totem silence
With face of wood refuses to testify.

The famous exile's dead, from many on many
Deportations, from Spain to Prague to Nice,
Kaleidoscopic police, his Dance Macabre;
One of the best the worst had never feared.

You, you I cherish with my learned heart
As in the bombed cathedral town, doubly
A tourist trophy now, the dean shouted: 'At last!
At least and at last we have stored the windows away.

The fabulation of my Lord's glory, by
Seven and by seven and by seven multiplied!'
So is my care though none your mystic I,
Nor you like the painted saints but breath and more.

And do not pace the room haunting the furniture
But be my insular love; and I would have you
Fingering the ring with its silver bat, the foreign
And credible Chinese symbol of happiness.

JANSENIST JOURNEY

'Then, We'll go through with the journey,' said
My brother and myself, 'and bring
With us our black-faced scapegoat, Guilt.'

We bested the last lingering hill
Of life; and got donkeys to ride
For it would be long going through the wood.

I was to loose our goat of guilt
At a shameful bypath on the way;
But the brightness turned him innocent:

The donkey's patience through the thorns,
The gay old nurses, the green inns:
He bucked the wild flowers with flashing horns:

These freshets garlic to his taste.
But I put no trust in him, no trust.
At last we reached the Gospel gates,

Aching and dirty. Robes lay there.
Mother and sisters like light through glass,
With stopped lightning stood in the arch.

They washed our heads, hands and feet,
In the same low voice they laughed and sobbed,
The mother gave us a diamond each,

Casketed, shut with a miser's clasp,
I said to my brother: 'Life, the diamond,
Is locked inside hard and fast.'

'Yes?' he said, putting his down
Indifferently. I opened mine:
It was a gold ball. It was sundown,

We entered cloisters with a priest,
Sat on the stone wall, listening
To his plans for our retreat,

Black-face forgotten, the diamond too,
And the mother and sisters. No rapture;
The plain virtue of the chosen few.

THE PASSION OF CHRIST

to Allen Tate

THE FALL
From what did man fall?
From the Archangel Michael's irritated wing?
Man is so small,
Without him first the universe did sing,
So fortunate since the Christ endued his caul:
Let us take on the whole
Story in its negligence and passion—
Archangel, we your images that fall,
Dissolve and reassemble, session by session.
You rise and rise, God's wasp, and sting!
We fall and rise, God's instrument, and sing!

THE GARDEN OF EDEN
Leaving the Garden, our first father stayed
Behind, and wept, and death is still delayed.

THE MAN OF SORROWS
He sought our sorrow out and brought it back
From merchants in the back streets of the heart:
But we, suspended between love and lack,
    Will neither sign off nor take part.

THE ANNUNCIATION
What we have best imagined is the Mother
Who, with the absolute, say Light, brought forth
Self, without intervention of the Other,
    The pure, the Virgin birth.

Gabriel, death-borne on shaking, human knees,
Humorously settles down,
Deriding with his infinite, mad eyes
    Our market risk, our saints' unknown.

THE NATIVITY
We are told how the Son of Man was born,
    Known to His Father, Who never
Recognises birth or death; and how the worn
    World's to be His breath forever.

CHRIST TAKES LEAVE OF HIS MOTHER
He, Who was born of Her that knew not Nature,
Yet with shut fists weeps like Nature's creature;
The black skies resent their shuddering wings,
And what was heavenly weeps, what natural sings.

CHRIST'S ENTRY INTO JERUSALEM
Open the gates and welcome in the Lord!
His sweet brow and invisible sword.

Now the palms wither, and the arch
Befriends no more the trulls' and porters' march.

Caesar takes the show seriously —
But Christ is serious with a world to free.

CHRIST EXPELS THE MERCHANTS FROM THE TEMPLE
The salesmen of ideas fake their list,
Worse than the trulls and their traffickers!
Again and again He strikes them off the list —
Again and again they claim the place as theirs.

WASHING OF THE FEET
With false and annual humility,
Contracting singular love into its type,
The Pharisees extend their feet, which He
In saintly rage will wash, and even wipe!

THE LAST SUPPER
None of us can remember without tears
Nor asking with what faculty we failed:
Was it the purse, or Peter's doubting ears?
        Or the rash brethren jailed?

And when Judas wiped his mouth with bread:
What horror was it raised our loyal arm?
The small room was filled with all the dead;
And Christ broke bread and broke the mortal charm.

Outside the window, the world was still,
Absence of principalities and powers:
        The world His will,
He broke bread and said He would be ours.

THE AGONY IN THE GARDEN
Peter and James and John.
Though the fox find shelter and the swollen famished dog
And in His dispensation sleep the innocent log,
Yet the Lord finds no breast to lean upon.

Peter and James and John.
Olive branches mime against the moonlight
All natural agitation from sound to sight:
Yet there is not pain enough in Nature for Him to
        reason on.

Peter and James and John.
It is not angels He wants, nor fallen angels even,
        but men
To wear down, if only in Time, that unnatural pain;
Not active Peter, nor neutral James, nor passive John.

CHRIST BEFORE THE MAGISTRATES
By now the Church and State have had their fling,
The generous flesh is pared to the bone:
Christ and Caesar come to the same thing,
        The scorned and scornful soul, their own.

There will be something more when this is over,
The Lion and the Lamb adopt His voice,
        Beloved submit to lover,
Kneel down, and then stand up and rejoice!

VERONICA'S VEIL
They tend His fierce divinity, shy saviours,
From the calvaries of the dispossessed,
Ragged mothers who give milk to their neighbours
While the husband fails, and the child undressed

Scrabbles at the empty plate, some holy women
Will take their last white linen from the drawer
And saying: 'God is ours as He is human,'
Wipe the blood from the unbearable scar.

BEFORE PILATE
To flagellate, to crown with thorns, to make
A show of man who would Man create —
Nothing much when Justice is at stake —
The conflict of laws idly becomes Fate.

The scene's complete! the filthy, wine-lit bands
Forgive Barabbas who shed blood,
Pilate, the surgeon, cleans his distant hands,
In sage disgust, praises the Good.

WAY OF THE CROSS
At every stage along that station,
Averted eyes, reluctant heart!
Mob hatred, Pharisees' elation —
His knees watery from the start,

One, Simon, in excess of passion,
Trusted his unreflecting hands;
What is this genius of compassion
That comprehends, nor understands!

AT CALVARY
Axes shone in the sunlight
Where sound and sight from one source came;
Christ was striking at the roots
Whence grew our birthright and its name,

The reason that was perfect gave
The round, simple, pagan sun:
What was humanity to save
The tears of Christ in the machine?

LIFTED ON THE CROSS
There's little certain — but no doubt
Eternity in Time's put out!

There may be lights over the plain,
That's where some acolytes, mad and sane,

Mad for life and sane for death:
Centurion! crown these ribs of wrath!

THE CROSS
Two thieves — why two? to make three criminals?
How dare the centre judge the left and right
Judging: 'You shall be with Me in Paradise'
Judging: 'You shall be in Hell for life'
If I were one of those two casual thieves
And spied on our degraded bloody Lord:
How could I know how to pronounce the Word,
The Word that doubts, the Word that believes?

THE GOOD THIEF
It is not right for me to talk to You,
To wait on You with ministerial bow,
To pray, or if I lived in higher merit
To love even, or to adore, or care.
Why? the reasons? there are many of them;
    That You are there and are not there.

The huge and foreign universes round me,
The small dishonours in me coat my heart:
Whether the whim of the ignoble beast
Or the Gothic nobility of the choir,
It makes no difference, both high and low,
    Are burned to nothing in Your fire.

My will You will for a fire towards You
Dies without my kindling, or is quenched
In unguided storms from Your high quarters:
My memory in lethargy turns sour
All whence, my understanding less imperious
    Day by day and hour by hour,

Loses whole continents where in my childhood
I was Your Viceroy, and approved the Just
And condemned my natural evil thoughts —
Now, what has changed me? Is it the years
You made and gave me, Lord? or am I prone to the evil
    The masters dinned into my ears?

Praise and recrimination sit well on us
Whose quality's defined by life and death;
But nothing, neither life or death adorns us

Like adoration of our Lord, the Christ,
No buildings, no culture of roses, no bridges
    Like the majesty of Christ.

THE BAD THIEF
Lord, we You've made it in our power
To destroy the World You saved us in
And not only our bodies with Your souls,
Your soul created for Your praise forever
But all that has been made against Your image
    Passes, both now and never,

Beasts that eat their young in innocence,
Men that torture knowing what they do —
Innocent things and conscientious things —
We who destroy the flower and the grass,
The thrush whose song's as powerful as the sea
    All this and more has come to pass.

ASCENSION
It happens through the blond window, the trees
With diverse leaves divide the light, light birds;
Aengus, the God of Love, my shoulders brushed
With birds, you could say lark or thrush or thieves

And not be right yet — or ever right —
For it was God's Son foreign to our moor:
When I looked out the window, all was white,
And what's beloved in the heart was sure,

With such a certainty ascended He,
The Son of Man who deigned Himself to be:
Then when we lifted out of sleep, there was
Life with its dark, and love above the laws.

TRANSFIGURATION
All is as if that Face transpired with Light
As if dark were light
As if wrong were right
The torsion and the tension of that Night!

The world opens like a door: Come in!
Body is in the way,
Soul is waste and play,
Oh, come, Unworldly, from the World within!

LOUGH DERG

The poor in spirit on their rosary rounds,
The jobbers with their whiskey-angered eyes,
The pink bank clerks, the tip-hat papal counts,
And drab, kind women their tonsured mockery tries,
Glad invalids on penitential feet
Walk the Lord's majesty like their village street.

With mullioned Europe shattered, this Northwest,
Rude-sainted isle would pray it whole again:
(Peasant Apollo! Troy is worn to rest.)
Europe that humanized the sacred bane
Of God's chance who yet laughed in his mind
And balanced thief and saint: were they this kind?

Low rocks, a few weasels, lake
Like a field of burnt gorse; the rooks caw;
Ours, passive, for man's gradual wisdom take
Firefly instinct dreamed out into law;
The prophets' jeweled kingdom down at heel
Fires no Augustine here. Inert, they kneel;

All is simple and symbol in their world,
The incomprehended rendered fabulous.
Sin teases life whose natural fruits withheld
Sour the deprived nor bloom for timely loss:
Clan Jansen! less what magnanimity leavens
Man's wept-out, fitful, magniloquent heavens

Where prayer was praise, O Lord! the Temple trumpets
Cascaded down Thy sunny pavilions of air,
The scroll-tongued priests, the galvanic strumpets,
All clash and stridency gloomed upon Thy stair;
The pharisees, the exalted boy their power
Sensually psalmed in Thee, their coming hour!

And to the sun, earth turned her flower of sex,
Acanthus in the architects' limpid angles;
Close priests allegorized the Orphic egg's
Brood, and from the Academy, tolerant wranglers
Could hear the contemplatives of the Tragic Choir
Drain off man's sanguine, pastoral death-desire.

It was said stone dreams and animal sleeps and man
Is awake; but sleep with its drama on us bred
Animal articulate, only somnambulist can
Conscience like Cawdor give the blood its head
For the dim moors to reign through druids again.
O first geometer! tangent-feelered brain

Clearing by inches the encircled eyes,
Bolder than the peasant tiger whose autumn beauty
Sags in the expletive kill, or the sacrifice
Of dearth puffed positive in the stance of duty
With which these pilgrims would propitiate
Their fears; no leafy, medieval state

Of paschal cathedrals backed on earthy hooves
Against the craftsmen's primary-coloured skies
Whose gold was Gabriel on the patient roofs,
The parabled windows taught the dead to rise,
And Christ the Centaur, in two natures whole,
With fable and proverb joinered body and soul.

Water withers from the oars. The pilgrims blacken
Out of the boats to masticate their sin
Where Dante smelled among the stones and bracken
The door to Hell (O harder Hell where pain
Is earthed, a casuist sanctuary of guilt!).
Spirit bureaucracy on a bet built

Part by this race when monks in convents of coracles
For the Merovingian centuries left their land,
Belled, fragrant; and honest in their oracles
Bespoke the grace to give without demand,
Martyrs Heaven winged nor tempted with reward.
And not ours, doughed in dogma, who never have dared

Will with surrogate palm distribute hope:
No better nor worse than I who, in my books,
Have angered at the stake with Bruno and, by the rope
Watt Tyler swung from, leagued with shifty looks
To fuse the next rebellion with the desperate
Serfs in the sane need to eat and get;

Have praised, on its thunderous canvas, the Florentine smile
As man took to wearing his death, his own
Sapped crisis through cathedral branches (while
Flesh groped loud round dissenting skeleton)
In soul, reborn as body's appetite:
Now languisht back in body's amber light,

Now is consumed. O earthly paradise!
Hell is to know our natural empire used
Wrong, by mind's moulting, brute divinities.
The vanishing tiger's saved, his blood transfused.
Kent is for Jutes again and Glasgow town
Burns high enough to screen the stars and moon.

Well may they cry who have been robbed, their wasting
Shares in justice legally lowered until
Man his own actor, matrix, mold and casting,
Or man, God's image, sees his idol spill.
Say it was pride that did it, or virtue's brief:
To them that suffer it is no relief.

All indiscriminate, man, stone, animal
Are woken up in nightmare. What John the Blind
From Patmos saw works and we speak it. Not all
The men of God nor the priests of mankind
Can mend or explain the good and broke, not one
Generous with love prove communion.

Behind the eyes the winged ascension flags,
For want of spirit by the market blurbed,
And if hands touch, such fraternity sags
Frightened this side the dykes of death disturbed
Like Aran Islands' bibulous, unclean seas:
Pietà: but the limbs ache; it is not peace.

Then to see less, look little, let hearts' hunger
Feed on water and berries. The pilgrims sing:
Life will fare well from elder to younger,
Though courage fail in a world-end, rosary ring.
Courage kills its practitioners and we live,
Nothing forgotten, nothing to forgive.

We pray to ourself. The metal moon, unspent
Virgin eternity sleeping in the mind,
Excites the form of prayer without content;
Whitethorn lightens, delicate and blind,
The negro mountain, and so, knelt on her sod,
This woman beside me murmuring *My God! My God!*

RICHARD MURPHY
(1927-   )

SAILING TO AN ISLAND

The boom above my knees lifts, and the boat
Drops, and the surge departs, departs, my cheek
Kissed and rejected, kissed, as the gaff sways
A tangent, cuts the infinite sky to red
Maps, and the mast draws eight and eight across
Measureless blue, the boatmen sing or sleep.

We point all day for our chosen island,
Clare, with its crags purpled by legend:
There under castles the hot O'Malleys,
Daughters of Granuaile, the pirate queen
Who boarded a Turk with a blunderbuss,
Comb red hair and assemble cattle.
Across the shelved Atlantic groundswell
Plumbed by the sun's kingfisher rod,
We sail to locate in sea, earth and stone
The myth of a shrewd and brutal swordswoman
Who piously endowed an abbey.
Seven hours we try against the wind and tide,
Tack and return, making no headway.
The north wind sticks like a gag in our teeth.

Encased in a mirage, steam on the water,
Loosely we coast where hideous rocks jag
An acropolis of cormorants, an extinct
Volcano where spiders spin, a purgatory
Guarded by hags and bristled with breakers.

The breeze as we plunge slowly stiffens:
There are hills of sea between us and land,
Between our hopes and the island harbour.
A child vomits. The boat veers and bucks

There is no refuge on the gannet's cliff.
We are far, far out: the hull is rotten,
The spars are splitting, the rigging is frayed,
And our helmsman laughs uncautiously.
What of those who must earn their living

On the ribald face of a mad mistress?
We in holiday fashion know
This is the boat that belched its crew
Dead on the shingle in the Cleggan disaster.

Now she dips, and the sail hits the water.
She luffs to a squall; is struck; and shudders.
Someone is shouting. The boom, weak as scissors,
Has snapped. The boatman is praying.
Orders thunder and canvas cannonades.
She smothers in spray. We still have a mast;
The oar makes a boom. I am told to cut
Cords out of fishing-lines, fasten the jib.
Ropes lash my cheeks. Ease! Ease at last:
She swings to leeward, we can safely run.
Washed over rails our Clare Island dreams,
With storm behind us we straddle the wakeful
Waters that draw us headfast to Inishbofin.

The bows rock as she overtakes the surge.
We neither sleep nor sing nor talk,
But look to the land where the men are mowing.
What will the islanders think of our folly?

The whispering spontaneous reception committee
Nods and smokes by the calm jetty.
Am I jealous of these courteous fishermen
Who hand us ashore, for knowing the sea
Intimately, for respecting the storm
That took nine of their men on one bad night
And five from Rossadillisk in this very boat?
Their harbour is sheltered. They are slow to tell
The story again. There is local pride
In their home-built ships.
We are advised to return next day by the mail.

But tonight we stay, drinking with people
Happy in the monotony of boats,
Bringing the catch to the Cleggan market,
Cultivating fields, or retiring from America
With enough to soak till morning or old age.

The bench below my knees lifts, and the floor
Drops, and the words depart, depart, with faces
Blurred by the smoke. An old man grips my arm,
His shot eyes twitch, quietly dissatisfied.
He has lost his watch, an American gold
From Boston gas-works. He treats the company
To the secretive surge, the sea of his sadness.
I slip outside, fall among stones and nettles,
Crackling dry twigs on an elder tree,
While an accordion drones above the hill.

Later, I reach a room, where the moon stares
Cob-webbed through the window. The tide has ebbed,
Boats are careened in the harbour. Here is a bed.

THE WOMAN OF THE HOUSE
In memory of my grandmother Lucy Mary Ormsby
whose home was in the west of Ireland 1873-1958

On a patrician evening in Ireland
I was born in the guest-room: she delivered me.
May I deliver her from the cold hand
Where now she lies, with a brief elegy?

It was her house where we spent holidays,
With candles to bed, and ghostly stories:
In the lake of her heart we were islands
Where the wild asses galloped in the wind.

Her mind was a vague and log-warmed yarn
Spun between sleep and acts of kindliness:
She fed our feelings as dew feeds the grass
On April nights, and our mornings were green:

And those happy days, when in spite of rain
We'd motor west where the salmon-boats tossed,
She would sketch on the pier among the pots
Waves in a sunset, or the rising moon.

Indian-meal porridge and brown soda-bread,
Boiled eggs and buttermilk, honey from gorse,

Far more than we wanted she always offered
In a heart-surfeit: she ate little herself.

Mistress of mossy acres and unpaid rent,
She crossed the walls on foot to feed the sick:
Though frugal cousins frowned on all she spent
People had faith in her healing talent.

She bandaged the wounds that poverty caused
In the house that famine labourers built,
Gave her hands to cure impossible wrong
In a useless way, and was loved for it.

Hers were the fruits of a family tree:
A china clock, the Church's calendar,
Gardeners polite, governesses plenty,
And incomes waiting to be married for.

How the feckless fun would flicker her face
Reading our future by cards at the fire,
Rings and elopements, love-letters, old lace,
A signet of jokes to seal our desire.

'It was sad about Maud, poor Maud!' she'd sigh,
To think of the friend she lured and teased
Till she married the butler. 'Starved to death,
No service either by padre or priest.'

Cholera raged in the Residency;
'They kept my uncle alive on port.'
Which saved him to slaughter a few sepoys
And retire to Galway in search of sport.

The pistol that lost an ancestor's duel,
The hoof of the horse that carried him home
To be stretched on chairs in the drawing-room,
Hung by the Rangoon prints and the Crimean medal.

Lever and Lover, Somerville and Ross
Have fed the same worm as Blackstone and Gibbon,
The mildew has spotted *Clarissa's* spine
And soiled the *Despatches of Wellington.*

Beside her bed lay an old Bible that
Her Colonel Rector husband used to read,
And a new *Writers' and Artists' Year-book*
To bring a never-printed girlhood back.

The undeveloped thoughts died in her head,
But from her heart, through the people she loved
Images spread, and intuitions lived,
More than the mere sense of what she said.

At last, her warmth made ashes of the trees
Ancestors planted, and she was removed
To hospital to die there, certified.
Her house, but not her kindness, has found heirs.

Compulsory comforts penned her limping soul:
With all she uttered they smiled and agreed.
When she summoned the chauffeur, no one obeyed,
But a chrome hearse was ready for nightfall.

'Order the car for nine o'clock tonight!
I must get back, get back. They're expecting me.
I'll bring the spiced beef and the nuts and fruit.
Come home and I'll brew you lime-flower tea!

'The house in flames and nothing is insured!
Send for the doctor, let the horses go.
The dogs are barking again. Has the cow
Calved in the night? What is that great singed bird?

'I don't know who you are, but you've kind eyes.
My children are abroad and I'm alone.
They left me in this gaol. You all tell lies.
You're not my people. My people have gone.'

Now she's spent everything: the golden waste
Is washed away, silent her heart's hammer.
The children overseas no longer need her,
They are like aftergrass to her harvest.

People she loved were those who worked the land
Whom the land satisfied more than wisdom:
They've gone, a tractor ploughs where horses strained,
Sometimes sheep occupy their roofless room.

Through our inheritance all things have come,
The form, the means, all by our family:
The good of being alive was given through them,
We ourselves limit that legacy.

The bards in their beds once beat out ballads
Under leaky thatch listening to sea-birds,
But she in the long ascendancy of rain
Served biscuits on a tray with ginger wine.

Time can never relax like this again,
She in her phaeton looking for folk-lore,
He writing sermons in the library
Till lunch, then fishing all the afternoon.

On a wet winter evening in Ireland
I let go her hand, and we buried her
In the family earth beside her husband
Only to think of her, now warms my mind.

THE LAST GALWAY HOOKER

Where the Corrib river chops through the Claddagh
To sink in the tide-race its rattling chain
The boatwright's hammer chipped across the water

Ribbing this hooker, while a reckless gun
Shook the limestone quay-wall, after the Treaty
Had brought civil war to this fisherman's town.

That 'tasty' carpenter from Connemara, Cloherty,
Helped by his daughter, had half-planked the hull
In his eightieth year, when at work he died,

And she did the fastening, and caulked her well,
The last boat completed with old Galway lines.
Several seasons at the drift-nets she paid

In those boom-years, working by night in channels
With trammel and spillet and an island crew,
Tea-stew on turf in the pipe-black forecastle,

Songs of disasters wailed on the quay
When the tilt of the water heaves the whole shore.
'She was lucky always the *Ave Maria*',

With her brown barked sails, and her hull black tar,
Her forest of oak ribs and the larchwood planks,
The cavern-smelling hold bulked with costly gear,

Fastest in the race to the gull-marked banks,
What harbour she hived in, there she was queen
And her crew could afford to stand strangers drinks,

Till the buyers failed in nineteen twenty-nine,
When the cheapest of fish could find no market,
Were dumped overboard, the price down to nothing,

Until to her leisure a fisher priest walked
By the hungry dockside, full of her name,
Who made a cash offer, and the owners took it.

Then like a girl given money and a home
With no work but pleasure for her man to perform
She changed into white sails, her hold made room

For hammocks and kettles, the touch and perfume
Of priestly hands. So now she's a yacht
With pitch-pine spars and Italian hemp-ropes,

Smooth-running ash-blocks expensively bought
From chandlers in Dublin, two men get jobs
Copper-painting her keel and linseeding her throat,

While at weekends, nephews and nieces in mobs
Go sailing on picnics to the hermit islands,
Come home flushed with health having hooked a few dabs.

Munich, submarines, and the war's demands
Of workers to feed invaded that party
Like fumes of the diesel the dope of her sails,

When the Canon went east into limed sheep-lands
From the stone and reed patches of lobstermen
Having sold her to one on Cleggan Quay,

Who was best of the boatsmen from Inishbofin,
She his best buy. He shortened the mast, installed
A new 'Ailsa Craig', made a hold of her cabin,

Poured over the deck thick tar slightly boiled;
Every fortnight he drained the sump in the bilge
'To preserve the timbers'. All she could do, fulfilled.

The sea, good to gamblers, let him indulge
His fear when she rose winding her green shawl
And his pride when she lay calm under his pillage:

And he never married, was this hooker's lover,
Always ill-at-ease in houses or on hills,
Waiting for weather, or mending broken trawls:

Bothered by women no more than by the moon,
Not concerned with money beyond the bare need,
In this boat's bows he sheathed his life's harpoon.

A neap-tide of work, then a spring of liquor
Were the tides that alternately pulled his soul,
Now on a pitching deck with nets to hand-haul,

Then passing Sunday propped against a barrel
Winding among words like a sly helmsman
Till stories gathered around him in a shoal.

She was Latin blessed, holy water shaken
From a small whiskey bottle by a surpliced priest,
Madonnas wafered on every bulkhead,

Oil-grimed by the diesel, and her luck lasted
Those twenty-one years of skill buoyed by prayers,
Strength forged by dread from his drowned ancestors.

She made him money and again he lost it
In the fisherman's fiction of turning farmer:
The cost of timber and engine spares increased,

Till a phantom hurt him, ribs on a shore,
A hull each tide rattles that will never fish,
Sunk back in the sand, a story finished.

We met here last summer, nineteen fifty-nine,
Far from the missiles, the moon-shots, the money,
And we drank looking out on the island quay.

When his crew were in London drilling a motorway,
Old age had smoothed his barnacled will
And with wild songs he sold me the *Ave Maria.*

Then he was alone, stunned like a widower —
Relics and rowlocks pronging from the wall,
A pot of boiling garments, winter everywhere,

Especially in his bones, watching things fall,
Hooks of three-mile spillets, trammels at the foot
Of the unused double-bed — his mind threaded with all

The marline of his days twined within that boat,
His muscles' own shackles then staying the storm
Which now snap to bits like frayed thread.

So I chose to renew her, to rebuild, to prolong
For a while the spliced yards of yesterday.
Carpenters were enrolled, the ballast and the dung

Of cattle he'd carried lifted from the hold,
The engine removed, and the stale bilge scoured.
De Valera's daughter hoisted the Irish flag

At her freshly adzed mast this Shrove Tuesday,
Stepped while afloat between the tackle of the *Topaz*
And the *St. John,* by Bofin's best boatsmen,

All old as himself. Her skilful sailmaker,
Her inherited boatwright, her dream-tacking steersman
Picked up the tools of their interrupted work,

And in memory's hands this hooker was restored.
Old men my instructors, and with all new gear
May I handle her well down tomorrow's sea-road.

THE BATTLE OF AUGHRIM

I NOW

ON BATTLE HILL
Who owns the land where musket-balls are buried
In blackthorn roots on the eskar, the drained bogs
Where sheep browse, and credal war miscarried?
Names in the rival churches are written on plaques.

Behind the dog-rose ditch, defended with pikes,
A tractor sprays a rood of flowering potatoes:
Morning fog is lifting, and summer hikers
Bathe in a stream passed by cavalry traitors.

A Celtic cross by the road commemorates no battle
But someone killed in a car, Minister of Agriculture.
Dairy lorries on the fast trunk-route rattle:
A girl cycles along the lane to meet her lover.

Flies gyrate in their galaxy above my horse's head
As he ambles and shies close to the National School —
Bullets under glass, Patrick Sarsfield's *Would to God...*
And jolts me bareback on the road for Battle Hill:

Where a farmer with a tinker woman hired to stoop
Is thinning turnips by hand, while giant earth-movers
Shovel and claw a highway over the rector's glebe:
Starlings worm the aftergrass, a barley crop silvers,

And a rook tied by the leg to scare flocks of birds
Croaks as I dismount at the death-cairn of St. Ruth:
Le jour est á nous, mes enfants, his last words:
A cannonball beheaded him, and sowed a myth.

GREEN MARTYRS
I dream of a headless man
Sitting on a charger, chiselled stone.

A woman is reading from an old lesson:
'... who died in the famine.

Royal bulls on my land,
I starved to feed the absentee with rent.

Aughrim's great disaster
Made him two hundred years my penal master.

Rapparees, whiteboys, volunteers, ribbonmen,
Where have they gone?

Coerced into exile, scattered
Leaving a burnt gable and a field of ragwort.'

July the Twelfth, she takes up tongs
To strike me for a crop of calf-bound wrongs.

Her weekly half-crowns have built
A grey cathedral on the old gaol wall.

She brings me from Knock shrine
John Kennedy's head on a china dish.

ORANGE MARCH
In bowler hats and Sunday suits,
Orange sashes, polished boots,
Atavistic trainbands come
To blow the fife and beat the drum.

Apprentices uplift their banner
True blue-dyed with 'No Surrender!'
Claiming Aughrim as if they'd won
Last year, not 1691.

On Belfast silk, Victoria gives
Bibles to kneeling Zulu chiefs.
Read the moral, note the date:
'The secret that made Britain great.'

Derry, oakwood of bright angels,
Londonderry, dingy walls
Chalked at night with 'Fuck the Queen!'
Bygone canon, bygone spleen.

CASEMENT'S FUNERAL
After the noose, and the black diary deeds
Gossiped, his fame roots in prison lime:
The hanged bones burn, a revolution seeds.
Now Casement's skeleton is flying home.

A gun salutes, the troops slow-march, our new
Nation atones for her shawled motherland
Whose welcome gaoled him when a U-boat threw
This rebel quixote soaked on Banna Strand.

Soldiers in green guard the draped catafalque
With chalk remains of once ambiguous bone
Which fathered nothing till the traitor's dock
Hurt him to tower in legend like Wolfe Tone.

From gaol yard to the Liberator's tomb
Pillared in frost, they carry the freed ash,
Transmuted relic of a death-cell flame
Which purged for martyrdom the diarist's flesh.

On the small screen I watch the packed cortège
Pace from High Mass. Rebels in silk hats now
Exploit the grave with an old comrade's speech:
White hair tossed, a black cape flecked with snow.

HISTORICAL SOCIETY
I drive to a symposium
    On Ireland's Jacobite war,
Our new elite in a barrack-room
    Tasting vintage terror.

Once an imperial garrison
    Drank here to a king:
Today's toast is republican,
    We sing 'A Soldier's Song'.

One hands me a dinted musket-ball
    Heated by his palm.
'I found this bullet at Aughrim
    Lodged in a skull.'

SLATE
Slate I picked from a nettlebed
Had history, my neighbour said.

To quarry it, men had to row
Five miles, twelve centuries ago.

An inch thick, it hung watertight
Over monks' litany by candlelight:

Till stormed by viking raids, it slipped.
Four hundred years overlapped.

Pirates found it and roofed a fort
A mile west, commanding the port.

Red-clawed choughs perched on it saw
Guards throw priests to the sea's jaw.

Repaired to succour James the Shit
The battle of Aughrim shattered it.

Through centuries of penal gale
Hedge-scholars huddled where it fell.

Pegged above a sea-wormed rafter
It rattled over landlord's laughter.

Windy decades pined across
Barrack roof, rebellion, moss.

This week I paved my garden path
With slate St. Colman nailed on lath.

INHERITANCE
Left a Cromwellian demesne
My kinsman has bulldozed three bronze age raths

I remember a child fell dead the moon
Her father cut hawthorn in those weird rings.

Will his wife's baby be stillborn?
He wants his park to graze one beast per rood.

No tree can survive his chainsaw:
Hewing is part of the land reclamation scheme.

He's auctioned grandfather's Gallipoli sword
And bought a milking machine.

Slate he stripped from a Church of Ireland steeple
Has broadened his pig-sty roof:

Better a goat's hoof in the aisle
Than a rosary beads or electric guitars.

Five hundred cars pass the stone lion gates
For a civil war veteran's funeral.

On a grave behind a petrol pump
The wind wraps a newspaper around an obelisk.

On ancient battleground neat painted signs
Announce 'Gouldings Grows'.

CHRISTENING
A side-car creaks on the gravel drive,
The quality arrive.

With Jordan water
They mean to give me a Christian start.

Harmonium pedals squeak and fart.
I'm three weeks old.

It's a garrison world:
The good are born into the Irish gentry.

What do they hope my use of life will be?
Duty.

Fight the good fight:
Though out of tune, if loud enough, it's right.

Under the Holy Table there's a horse's skull
Shot for a landlord's funeral:

From a religious duel
The horse cantered the wounded master home.

Two clergy christen me: I'm saved from Rome.
The deaf one has not heard my name,

He thinks I am a girl.
The other bellows: 'It's a boy, you fool!'

HISTORY
One morning of arrested growth
An army list roll-called the sound
Of perished names, but I found no breath
In dog-eared inventories of death.

Touch unearths military history.
Sifting clay on a mound, I find
Bones and bullets fingering my mind:
The past is happening today.

The battle cause, a hand grenade
Lobbed in a playground, the king's viciousness
With slaves succumbing to his rod and kiss,
Has a beginning in my blood.

SEALS AT HIGH ISLAND

The calamity of seals begins with jaws.
Born in caverns that reverberate
With endless malice of the sea's tongue
Clacking on shingle, they learn to bark back
In fear and sadness and celebration.
The ocean's mouth opens forty feet wide
And closes on a morsel of their rock.

Swayed by the thrust and backfall of the tide,
A dappled grey bull and a brindled cow
Copulate in the green water of a cove.
I watch from a cliff-top, trying not to move.
Sometimes they sink and merge into black shoals;
Then rise for air, his muzzle on her neck,
Their winged feet intertwined as a fishtail.

She opens her fierce mouth like a scarlet flower
Full of white seeds; she holds it open long
At the sunburst in the music of their loving;
And cries a little. But I must remember
How far their feelings are from mine marooned.
If there are tears at this holy ceremony
Theirs are caused by brine and mine by breeze.

When the great bull withdraws his rod, it glows
Like a carnelian candle set in jade.
The cow ripples ashore to feed her calf;
While an old rival, eyeing the deed with hate,
Swims to attack the tired triumphant god.
They rear their heads above the boiling surf,
Their terrible jaws open, jetting blood.

At nightfall they haul out, and mourn the drowned,
Playing to the sea sadly their last quartet,
An improvised requiem that ravishes
Reason, while ripping scale up like a net:
Brings pity trembling down the rocky spine
Of headlands, till the bitter ocean's tongue
Swells in their cove, and smothers their sweet song.

WALKING ON SUNDAY

Walking on Sunday into Omey Island
   When the tide has fallen slack,
I crossed a spit of wet ribbed sand
   With a cold breeze at my back.

Two sheepdogs nosed me at a stile,
   Boys chevied on the green,
A woman came out of a house to smile
   And tell me she had seen

Men digging down at St. Fechin's church,
   Buried in sand for centuries
Up to its pink stone gable top, a perch
   For choughs and seapies.

I found a dimple scalloped from a dune
    A landing-slip for coracles,
Two graveyards — one for women, one for men—
    Odorous of miracles:

And twelve parishioners probing a soft floor
    To find what solid shape there was
Under shell-drift; seeking window, door;
    And measuring the house.

Blood was returning dimly to the face
    Of the chancel they'd uncovered,
Granite skin that rain would kiss
    Until the body flowered.

I heard the spades clang with a shock
    Inaugurating spring:
Fechin used plug and feather to split rock
    And poised the stone to sing.

He tuned cacophony to make
    Harmony in this choir:
The ocean gorged on it, he died of plague,
    And hawks nested there.

PAT CLOHERTY'S VERSION OF *THE MAISIE*

I've no tooth to sing you the song
    Tierney made at the time
        but I'll tell the truth

It happened on St. John's Day
    sixty-eight years ago
        last June the twenty-fourth

The Maisie sailed from Westport Quay
    homeward on a Sunday
        missing Mass to catch the tide

John Kerrigan sat at her helm
   Michael Barrett stood at her mast
      and Kerrigan's wife lay down below

The men were two stepbrothers
   drownings in the family
      and all through the family

Barrett kept a shop in the island
   Kerrigan plied the hooker
      now deeply laden with flour

She passed Clare and she came to Cahir
   two reefs tied in the mainsail
      she bore a foresail but no jib

South-east wind with strong ebb-tide
   still she rode   this way   that way
      hugging it   hugging it   O my dear

And it blew and blew hard and blew hard
   but Kerrigan kept her to it
      as long as he was there he kept her to it

Rain fell in a cloudburst
   hailstones hit her deck
      there was no return for him once he'd put out

At Inishturk when the people saw
   The Maisie smothered up in darkness
      they lit candles in the church

What more could Kerrigan do?
   he put her jaw into the hurricane
      and the sea claimed him

Barrett was not a sailor
   to take a man from the water
      the sea claimed him too

At noon the storm ceased
   and we heard *The Maisie*'d foundered
      high upon a Mayo strand

The woman came up from the forecastle
   she came up alone on deck
      and a great heave cast her out on shore

And another heave came while she drowned
   and put her on her knees
      like a person'd be in prayer

That's the way the people found her
   and the sea never came in
      near that mark no more

John Kerrigan was found
   far down at Achill Sound
      he's buried there

Michael Barrett was taken
   off Murrisk Pier
      he's buried there

Kerrigan's wife was brought from Cross
   home to Inishbofin
      and she's buried there

THE READING LESSON

Fourteen years old, learning the alphabet,
He finds letters harder to catch than hares
Without a greyhound. Can't I give him a dog
To track them down, or put them in a cage?
He's caught in a trap, until I let him go,
Pinioned by 'Don't you want to learn to read?'
'I'll be the same man whatever I do.'

He looks at a page as a mule balks at a gap
From which a goat may hobble out and bleat.
His eyes jink from a sentence like flushed snipe
Escaping shot. A sharp word, and he'll mooch
Back to his piebald mare and bantam cock.
Our purpose is as tricky to retrieve
As mercury from a smashed thermometer.

'I'll not read any more.' Should I give up?
His hands, long-fingered as a Celtic scribe's,
Will grow callous, gathering sticks or scrap;
Exploring pockets of the horny drunk
Loiterers at the fairs, giving them lice.
A neighbour chuckles. 'You can never tame
The wild-duck: when his wings grow, he'll fly off.'

If books resembled roads, he'd quickly read:
But they're small farms to him, fenced by the page,
Ploughed into lines, with letters drilled like oats:
A field of tasks he'll always be outside.
If words were bank-notes, he would filch a wad;
If they were pheasants, they'd be in his pot
For breakfast, or if wrens he'd make them king.

COPPERSMITH

A temple tree grew in our garden in Ceylon.
We knew it by no other name.
The flower, if you turned it upside down,
Looked like a dagoba with an onion dome.
A holy perfume
Stronger than the evil tang of betel-nut
Enticed me into its shade on the stuffiest afternoon,

Where I stood and listened to the tiny hammer-stroke
Of the crimson coppersmith perched above my head,
His *took took took*
And his *tonk tonk tonk*
Were spoken in a language I never understood:
And there I began to repeat
Out loud to myself an English word such as *beat beat beat,*

Till hammering too hard I lost the meaning in the sound
Which faded and left nothing behind,
A blank mind,
The compound spinning round,
My brain melting, as if I'd stood in the sun
Too long without a topee and was going blind,
Till I and the bird, the word and the tree, were one.

NOCTURNE

The blade of a knife
Is tapped gently on an oak table
Waves are sobbing in coves

Light bleeds on the sky's rim
From dusk till dawn
Petrels fly in from the ocean

Wings beating on stone
Quick vibrations of notes throats tongues
Under silverweed   calling and calling

Louder cries cut the air
They rise from a pit
Complaints are retched up and lost

A solo tune
Is dying with passion
For someone out there to come quickly

Come back   come back
I'm here   here   here
This burrow   this wall   this hole

Ach   who kept you?   where've you been?
There   there   there
It's all over   over   over

STORMPETREL

Gipsy of the sea
In winter wambling over scurvy whaleroads,
Jooking in the wake of ships,
A sailor hooks you
And carves his girl's name on your beak.

Guest of the storm
Who sweeps you off to party after party,
You flit in a sooty grey coat
Smelling of must
Barefoot across a sea of broken glass.

Waif of the afterglow
On summer nights to meet your mate you jink
Over sea-cliff and graveyard,
Creeping underground
To hatch an egg in a hermit's skull.

Pulse of the rock
You throb till daybreak on your cryptic nest
A song older than fossils,
Ephemeral as thrift.
It ends with a gasp.

TROUVAILLE

This root of bog-oak the sea dug up she found
Poking about, in old age, and put to stand
Between a snarling griffin and a half-nude man
Moulded of lead on my chimney-piece.
It looks like a heron rising from a pond,
Feet dipped in brown-trout water,
Head shooting arrow-sharp into blue sky.

'What does it remind you of?' she wanted to know.
I thought of trees in her father's demesne
Levelled by chainsaws;
Bunches of primroses I used to pick
Before breakfast, hunting along a limestone lane,
To put at her bedside before she woke;
And all my childhood's broken promises.

No, no! It precedes alphabets,
Planted woods, or gods.
Twisted and honed as a mind that never forgets
It lay dead in bog acids, undecayable:
Secretively hardening in a womb of moss, until
The peat burnt off, a freak tide raised
The feathered stick she took to lure me home.

CARE

Kidded in April above Glencolumbkille
On a treeless hill backing north, she throve
Sucking milk off heather and rock, until

I came with children to buy her. We drove
South, passing Drumcliff. Restless in the car,
Bleating, she gulped at plastic teats we'd shove

Copiously in her mouth. Soon she'd devour
Whatever we'd give. Prettily she poked
Her gypsy head with hornbuds through barbed wire

To nip off pea-tops, her fawn pelt streaked
With Black Forest shadow and Alpine snow.
I stalled her wildness in a pen that locked.

She grew tame and fat, fed on herbs I knew
Her body needed. We ransacked Kylemore
To bring her oakleaf, ivy and bark to chew.

I gutted goatbooks, learning how to cure
Fluke, pulpy kidney, black garget, louping ill:
All my attention bled to cope with her.

No fenceless commonage to roam, no hill
Transfigured into cloud, no dragon wood
To forage with a puck-led flock: but the rattle

Of a bucket, shouts of children bringing food
Across a frozen yard. Out in a forest
She would have known a bad leaf from a good.

Here, captive to our taste, she'd learnt to trust
The petting hand with crushed oats, or a new
Mash of concentrates, or sweet bits of waste.

So when a child mistook a sprig of yew
And mixed it with her fodder, she descried
No danger: we had tamed her instinct too.

Whiskey, white of egg, linseed oil, we tried
Forcing down antidotes. Nothing would do.
The children came to tell me when she died.

THOMAS KINSELLA
(1928-   )

MIDSUMMER

Hereabouts the signs are good.
Propitious creatures of the wood
    After their fashion
Have pitied and blessed before our eyes.
All unpremeditated lies
    Our scattered passion.

Flowers whose names I do not know
Make happy signals to us. O
    Did ever bees
Stumble on such a quiet before!
The evening is a huge closed door
    And no one sees

How we, absorbed in our own art,
Have locked ourselves inside one heart,
    Grown silent and,
Under beech and sacred larch,
Watched as though it were an arch
    That heart expand.

Something that for this long year
Had hid and halted like a deer
    Turned marvellous,
Parted the tragic grasses, tame,
Lifted its perfect head and came
    To welcome us.

We have, dear reason, of this glade
An endless tabernacle made,
    An origin.
Well for whatever lonely one
Will find this right place to lay down
    His desert in.

BAGGOT STREET DESERTA

Lulled, at silence, the spent attack.
The will to work is laid aside.
The breaking-cry, the strain of the rack,
Yield, are at peace. The window is wide
On a crawling arch of stars, and the night
Reacts faintly to the mathematic
Passion of a cello suite
Plotting the quiet of my attic.
A mile away the river toils
Its buttressed fathoms out to sea;
Tucked in the mountains, many miles
Away from its roaring outcome, a shy
Gasp of waters in the gorse
Is sonnetting origins. Dreamers' heads
Lie mesmerised in Dublin's beds
Flashing with images, Adam's morse.

A cigarette, the moon, a sigh
Of educated boredom, greet
A curlew's lingering threadbare cry
Of common loss. Compassionate,
I add my call of exile, half-
Buried longing, half-serious
Anger and the rueful laugh.
We fly into our risk, the spurious.

Versing, like an exile, makes
A virtuoso of the heart,
Interpreting the old mistakes
And discords in a work of Art
For the One, a private masterpiece
Of doctored recollections. Truth
Concedes, before the dew, its place
In the spray of dried forgettings Youth
Collected when they were a single
Furious undissected bloom.
A voice clarifies when the tingle
Dies out of the nerves of time:
Endure and let the present punish.
Looking backward, all is lost;
The Past becomes a fairy bog
Alive with fancies, double crossed

By pad of owl and hoot of dog,
Where shaven, serious-minded men
Appear with lucid theses, after
Which they don the mists again
With trackless, cotton-silly laughter;
Secretly a swollen Burke
Assists a decomposing Hare
To cart a body of good work
With midnight mutterings off somewhere;
The goddess who had light for thighs
Grows feet of dung and takes to bed,
Affronting horror-stricken eyes,
The marsh bird that children dread.

I nonetheless inflict, endure,
Tedium, intracordal hurt,
The sting of memory's quick, the drear
Uprooting, burying, prising apart
Of loves a strident adolescent
Spent in doubt and vanity.
All feed a single stream, impassioned
Now with obsessed honesty,
A tugging scruple that can keep
Clear eyes staring down the mile,
The thousand fathoms, into sleep.

Fingers cold against the sill
Feel, below the stress of flight,
The slow implosion of my pulse
In a wrist with poet's cramp, a tight
Beat tapping out endless calls
Into the dark, as the alien
Garrison in my own blood
Keeps constant contact with the main
Mystery, not to be understood.
Out where imagination arches
Chilly points of light transact
The business of the border-marches
Of the Real, and I — a fact
That may be countered or may not —
Find their privacy complete.

My quarter-inch of cigarette
Goes flaring down to Baggot Street.

THE LAUNDRESS

Her chair drawn to the door,
A basket at her feet,
She sat against the sun and stitched a linen sheet.
Over harrowed Flanders
August moved the wheat.

Poplars sharing the wind
With Saxony and France
Dreamed at her gate,
Soared in a Summer trance.
A cluck in the cobbled yard:
A shadow changed its stance.

As a fish disturbs the pond
And sinks without a stain
The heels of ripeness fluttered
Under her apron. Then
Her heart grew strained and light
As the shell that shields the grain.

Bluntly through the doorway
She stared at shed and farm,
At yellow fields unstitching
About the hoarded germ,
At land that would spread white
When she had reached her term.

The sower plumps his acre,
Flanders turns to the heat,
The winds of Heaven winnow
And the wheels grind the wheat.
She searched in her basket
And fixed her ruffled sheet.

COVER HER FACE

She has died suddenly, aged twenty-nine years, in Dublin.
Some of her family travel from the country to bring her body
home. Having driven all morning through a storm.

I
They dither softly at her bedroom door
In soaking overcoats, and words forsake
Even their comforters. The bass of prayer
Haunts the chilly landing while they take
Their places in a murmur of heartbreak.

Shabby with sudden tears, they know their part,
Mother and brother, resigning all that ends
At these drab walls. For here, with panicked heart,
A virgin broke the seal; who understands
The sheet pulled white and Maura's locked blue hands?

Later her frown will melt, when by degrees
They flinch from grief; a girl they have never seen,
Sunk now in love and horror to her knees,
The black official giving discipline
To shapeless sorrow, these are more their kin,

By grace of breath, than that grave derelict
Whose blood and feature, like a sleepy host,
Agreed a while with theirs. Her body's tact
Swapped child for woman, woman for a ghost,
Until its buried sleep lay uppermost;

And Maura, come to terms at last with pain
Rests in her ruptured mind, her temples tight,
Patiently weightless as her time burns down.
Soon her few glories will be shut from sight:
Her slightness, the fine metal of her hair spread out,

Her cracked, sweet laugh. Such gossamers as hold
Friends, family — all fortuitous conjunction —
Sever with bitter whispers; with untold
Peace shrivel to their anchors in extinction.
There, newly trembling, others grope for function.

II
Standing by the door, effaced in self,
I cannot deny her death, protest, nor grieve,
Dogged by a scrap of memory: some tossed shelf
Holds, a secret shared, that photograph,
Her arm tucked tiredly into mine; her laugh,

As though she also knew a single day
Would serve to bleed us to a diagram,
Sighs and confides; she waived validity
The night she drank the furnace of the Lamb,
Draining one image of its faint *I am.*

I watch her drift, in doubt whether dead or born
— Not with Ophelia's strewn virginity
But with a pale unmarriage — out of the worn
Bulk of day, under its sightless eye,
And close her dream in hunger. So we die.

Monday, without regret, darkens the pane
And sheds on the shaded living, the crystal soul,
A gloomy lustre of the pouring rain.
Nuns have prepared her for the holy soil
And round her bed the faded roses peel

That the fruit of justice may be sown in peace
To them that make peace, and bite its ashen bread.
Mother, brother, when our questions cease
Such peace may come, consenting to the good,
Chaste, biddable, out of all likelihood.

LANDSCAPE AND FIGURE

A man stoops low on the overcast plain. He is earthing
Or uprooting among heavy leaves. In the whole field
One dull poppy burns, on the drill by his boots.

The furrows yield themselves to his care. He does not
Lift his head; and would not, though the blight
Breathed on his fields out of the low clouds.

The blight breathes, or does not, invisibly,
As it will. Stalks still break into scattered flower.
Tissue forms about purpose as about seed.

He works toward the fruit of Adam. It darkens the plain,
Its seed a huge brain. The protecting flesh
When it falls will melt away in a kind of mud.

THE SECRET GARDEN

The place is growing difficult. Flails of bramble
Crawl into the lawn; on every hand
Glittering, toughened branches drink their dew.
Tiny worlds, drop by drop, tremble
On thorns and leaves; they will melt away.
The silence whispers around us:
Wither, wither, visible, invisible!

A child stands an instant at my knee.
His mouth smells of energy, light as light.
I touch my hand to his pearl flesh, taking strength.
He stands still, absorbing in return
The first taint. Immaculate, the waiting
Kernel of his brain.
How set him free, a son, toward the sour encounter?

Children's voices somewhere call his name.
He runs glittering into the sun, and is gone
... I cultivate my garden for the dew:
A rasping boredom funnels into death!
The sun climbs, a creature of one day,
And the dew dries to dust.
My hand strays out and picks off one sick leaf.

NIGHTWALKER

*The greater part must be content to be as though they had
not been.*

Mindful of the
    shambles of the day
But mindful, under the
    blood's drowsy humming,
Of will that gropes for
    structure — nonetheless
Not unmindful of
    the madness without,
The madness within (the
    book of reason slammed
Open, slammed shut)
    we presume to say:

I
I only know things seem and are not good.

A brain in the dark, and bones, out exercising
Shadowy flesh; fitness for the soft belly,
Fresh air for lungs that take no pleasure any longer.
The smell of gardens under suburban lamplight,
Clipped privet, a wall blotted with shadows
— Monsters of ivy squat in lunar glare.
              There, above the roofs,
It hangs, like a fat skull, or the pearl knob
Of a pendulum at the outermost reach of its swing,
Motionless. It is about to detach
Its hold on the upper night, for the return.
            Aye, I remember talk of it,
Though only a child. Not far from here it passed through
            — remorseless cratered face
Swift as the wind: a bludgeon tears free
From the world's bones, spikes breaking off
— Millions of little sharp limbs, jets of blood
Petrified in terror, jetted screams —
Then plunges upward far into the darkness —
            It meant little to me then,
Though I remember playing in the silence
When the rain of fragments dropped in the streets afterward
— Bone-splinters, silvery slivers of screams,

Blood-splinters rattling, like crimson flint.
                    There it hangs,
A mask of grey dismay sagging open
In the depths of torture, moron voiceless moon.
That dark area, the mark of Cain.

                              *

My shadow twists about my feet in the light
Of every passing street-lamp. Will-o'-the-wisp
In a bay window; a shadow slumped in the corner
Of a living-room, in blue trance, buried
Alive, two blank eyes. On a tiny screen
Mouths open and close, and bodies move
Obliquely and stoop, flickering —
                              embalmers
In eery light underground; their arms
Toil in silence.
                    A laboratory
Near Necropolis. It is midnight.
A shade enters,
                    patrolling the hive of his brain.
                    Window after window,
The same unearthly light consumes pitilessly.
Surely we can never die, sick spirits...
                    The minions stretch at rest,
Pale entities wound in a drowsy humming
At the brink of sleep. They snuggle in their cells
Faintly luminous, like grubs — abdominal
Body-juices and paper-thin shells, in their thousands,
In the smashable wax, o moon!
                              Musing thus,
I stroll upon my way, a vagabond
Tethered. My shadow twists at their feet.

                              *

I must lie down with them all soon and sleep,
And rise with them again when the new dawn
Has touched our pillows and our wet pallor
And roused us. We'll come scratching in our waistcoats
Down to the kitchen for a cup of tea;
Then with our briefcases, through wind or rain,
Past our neighbours' gardens — Melrose, Bloomfield —

To wait at the station, fluttering our papers,
Palping the cool wind discussing and murmuring.
                              Is it not right to serve
Our banks and businesses and government
As together we develop our community
On clear principles, with no fixed ideas?
And (twitching our thin umbrellas) acceptable
That during a transitional period
Development should express itself in forms
Without principle, based on fixed ideas —
                              Robed in spattered iron
At the harbour mouth she stands, Productive Investment,
And beckons the nations through our gold half-door:
Lend me your wealth, your cunning and your drive,
Your arrogant refuse;
                              let my people serve them
Bottled fury in our new hotels,
While native businessmen and managers
Drift with them, chatting, over to the window
To show them our growing city, give them a feeling
Of what is possible; our labour pool,
The tax concessions to foreign capital,
How to get a nice estate though German,
Even collect some of our better young artists.
                              Morose condemnation...
It is a weakness, and turns on itself.
                              Clean bricks
Are made of mud; we need them for our tower.

                              *

Spirit-skeletons are straggling into view
From the day's depths. You can pick them out
In the night sky, with a little patience:
                              Pale influences...
The wakeful Twins,
                              Bruder und Schwester
— Two young Germans I had in this morning
Wanting to transfer investment income;
The sister a business figurehead, her brother
Otterfaced, with exasperated smiles
Assuming — pressing until he achieved — response.
Handclasp; I do not exist; I cannot take
My eyes from their pallor. A red glare

Plays on their faces, livid with little splashes
Of blazing fat. The oven door closes.
                              All about and above me
The officials on the corridors or in their rooms
Work, or overwork, with mixed motives
Or none. We dwell together in urgency;
Dominate, entering middle age; subserve,
Aborting vague tendencies with buttery smiles.
Among us, behind locked doors, the ministers
Are working, with a sureness of touch found early
In the nation's birth — the blood of enemies
And brothers dried on their hide long ago.

Dragon old men, upright and stately and blind,
Or shuffling in the corridor finding a key,
Their youth cannot die in them; it will be found
Beating with violence when their bodies rot.
                              What occupies them
As they sit in their rooms? What they already are?
Shadow-flesh... claimed by pattern still living,
Linked into constellations with their dead...
                              Look! The Wedding Group:
The Groom, the Best Man, the Fox, and their three ladies
— A tragic tale: soon, the story tells,
Enmity sprang up between them, and the Fox
Took to the wilds. Then, to the Groom's sorrow,
His dear friend left him also, vowing hatred.
So they began destroying the Groom's substance
And he sent out to hunt the Fox, but trapped
His friend instead; mourning, he slaughtered him.
Shortly, in his turn, the Groom was savaged
On a Sunday morning, no one knows by whom.
And look, over here, in the same quarter,
The Two Executioners — Groom and Weasel —
'77' burning into each brow;
And look, the vivid Weasel there again,
Dancing crookbacked under the Player King
— A tragicomical tale:
                              how the Fox, long after,
Found a golden instrument one day,
A great complex gold horn, left at his door;
He examined it with little curiosity,

Wanting no gold or music, observed the mouthpiece,
Impossible to play with fox's lips,
And gave it with dull humour to his old enemy
The Weasel — who recognised the horn
Of the Player King, and bared his needle teeth.
He took it, hammered on it with a stick
And pranced about in blithe pantomime,
His head cocked to enjoy the golden clouts,
While the Fox from time to time nodded his mask.

II
The human taste grows faint,
                            It is gone,
Leaving a taste of self and laurel leaves
                    And rotted salt:
The gardens begin to smell of soaked sand
And half-stripped rocks in the dark. My bones obey
The sighing of the tide.
                            Another turning:
A cast-iron lamp-standard sheds yellow light
On the sea-wall; other lamps are lighting
Along a terrace of Victorian red-brick.
Big snails glisten among roots of iris.
Not a breath of wind. Joyce's Martello tower
Rises into the dark near the Forty Foot
On a prow frozen to stone.
                            Crossing the road
I hear my footsteps echo back from the terrace.
                            A sheet of newspaper
Gleams yellowish in the gutter. The morning *TIMES:*
Our new young minister glares from a photograph
— On horseback, in hunting pinks, from a low angle,
Haunch on haunch, Snigger, and by God...
                            The tide is drawing back
From the promenade, far as the lamplight can reach,
Trickling under the weed, into night's cave.
                            Note the silence.
Light never strays there. Nothing has a shadow there.
When a wind blows there...
                            A rustle in the gutter:
The hair stirs! Stealing over the waters,
Through the smell of seaweed, a spectral stink of horse
And rider's sweat...
                            What's that, outside the light?

*

Watcher in the tower, be with me now
At your parapet, above the glare of the lamps.
Turn your milky spectacles on the sea
Unblinking; cock your ear.
                    A rich darkness
Alive with signals: lights flash and wink;
Little bells clonk in the channel near the rocks;
Howth twinkles across the bay; ship-lights move
By invisible sea-lanes; the Baily light
Flickers, as it sweeps the middle darkness,
On some commotion...
                    A dripping cylinder
Big as a ship's funnel, pokes into sight,
Picked out by the moon. Two blazing eyes.
Then a whole head. Shoulders of shadowy muscle
Lit from within by joints and bones of light.
Another head... animal, with nostrils straining
Open, red as embers; goggle-eyes;
A spectral whinny! Forehoofs scrape at the night,
A rider grunts and urges.
                    Father of Authors!
It is himself! In silk hat and jowls,
Accoutred in stern jodhpurs! The sonhusband
Coming in his power: mounting to glory
On his big white harse!
                    He climbs the dark
To his mansion in the sky, to take his place
In the influential circle − a new sign:
                    Foxhunter.
                        Subjects will find
The going hard but rewarding. You may give offence
But this should pass. Marry the Boss's daughter.

The newspaper settles down in the gutter again:
                    THE ARCHBISHOP ON MARRIAGE
NEW MOVES TO RESTORE THE LANGUAGE
                        THE NEW IRELAND...
                    still awkward in the saddle
But able and willing for the foul ditch.
You'll sit as well as any at the kill,
Dark brother. What matter what iron Fausts
Open the gates?
                    It is begun: the curs
Mill and yelp at your heel, backsnapping and grinning.

They eye your back. Watch the smile of the dog.
They wait your signal, the kick of dirt in the teeth,
To turn them, in the old miracle,
To a pack of lickspittles running as one.

                              *

The foot of the tower. An angle where the darkness
Is complete. The parapet is empty.
A backdrop of constellations, crudely done
And mainly unfamiliar; they are arranged
To suggest a chart of the brain. Music   far off.
In the part of the little harbour that can be seen
The moon is reflected in low water.
Beyond, the lamps on the terrace.
                              The music fades.
                    Snuggle into the skull.
Total darkness wanders among my bones.
Lung-tips flutter. Wavelets lap the shingle.
From the vest's darkness, smell of my body:
                    Chalk dust and flowers...
Faint brutality. Shoes creak in peace.
Brother Burke flattens his soutane
Against the desk.
                    And the authorities
Used the National Schools to try to conquer
The Irish national spirit, at the same time
Exterminating what they called our 'jargon'
– The Irish language; in which Saint Patrick, Saint Bridget
And Saint Columcille taught and prayed!
Edmund Ignatius Rice founded our Order
To provide schools that were national in more than name:
Pupils from our schools played their part,
As you know, in the fight for freedom. And you will be called
In your different ways – to work for the native language,
To show your love by working for your country.
Today there are Christian Brothers' boys
Everywhere in the Government – the present Taoiseach
Sat where one of you is sitting now.
It wasn't long before Her Majesty
Gave us the famine – the starvation, as Bernard Shaw,
A godless writer, called it more accurately.
                    A hand is laid on my brow.
A voice breathes: You will ask are we struck dumb

By the unsimplifiable. Take these...
Bread of certainty; scalding soup of memories,
From my drowsy famine — martyrs in a dish
Of scalding tears: food of dragon men
And my own dragon half. Fierce pity!
                              The Blessed Virgin smiles
From her waxed pedestal, like young Victoria;
A green snake wriggles under her heel
Beside a vase of tulips.
                              Adolescents,
Celibates, we offer up our vows
To God and Ireland in Her name, grateful
That by our studies here they may not lack
Civil servants in a state of grace.
                              A glass partition rattles
In the draught. Rain against the windows.
A shiver clothes the flesh
                              bittersweet.
                              A seamew passes over,
Whingeing:
              Eire, Eire... is there none
To hear? Is all lost?
                              Not yet all; a while still
Your voice...
                              Alas, I think I will dash myself
At the stones, I will become a wind on the sea
Or a wave of the sea again, or a sea sound.
At the first light of the sun I stirred on my rock;
I have seen the sun go down at the end of the world;
Now I fly across the face of the moon.
                              A dying language echoes
Across a century's silence.
                              It is time,
Lost soul, I turned for home.
                              Sad music steals
Over the scene.
              Hesitant, cogitating, exit.

III
Home and beauty.
                    Her dear shadow on the blind,
The breadknife... She was slicing and buttering
A loaf of bread. My heart stopped. I starved for speech.
I believe now that love is half persistence,

A medium in which, from change to change,
Understanding may be gathered.
                              The return:
                    Virgin most pure, bright
In the dregs of the harbour: moon of my dismay,
Quiet as oil, enormous in her shaggy pool.
Her brightness, reflected on earth, in heaven,
Consumes my sight. Gradually, as my brain
At a great distance swims in the steady light,
Scattered notes, scraps of newspaper, photographs,
Begin to flow unevenly toward the pool
And gather into a book before her stare.
Her mask darkens as she reads, to my faint terror,
But she soon brightens a little, and smiles wanly:
                    It was a terrible time,
Nothing but sadness and horrors of one kind and another.
We came to take the waters. The sun shone brightly,
Which was very pleasant, and made it less gloomy,
Though my tears flowed again and again. When I drank
I felt my patience and trust coming back.
From time to time it seems that everything
Is breaking down; but we must never despair.
There are times it is all part of a meaningful drama
That begins in the grey mists of antiquity
And reaches through the years to unknown goals
In the consciousness of man, which is very soothing.
                    A wind sighs. The pool
Shivers: the tide at the turn. Odour of lamplight,
Sour soil, the sea bed, passes like a ghost
— The hem of her invisible garment.
                              Our mother
Rules on high, queenlike, pale with control.
                              Hatcher of peoples!
Incline from your darkness into mine!
I stand at the ocean's edge, my head fallen back
Heavy with your control, and oppressed!

                              *

That mad stare — the pulse hisses in my ear —
I am an arrow piercing the void, unevenly
As I correct and correct, but swift as thought.
I arrive, enveloped in blinding silence.
                              No wind stirs

On the dust floor. Far as the eye can see
Rock needles stand up from the plain; the horizon
A ring of sharp mountains like broken spikes.
Hard bluish light beats down, to kill
Any bodily thing — but a million dead voices hide
From it in the dust, without hope of peace.
(A cloud bursts from the ground, rock fragments scatter
In total silence.) A true desert, naked
To every peril. The shadows are alive:
They scuttle and flicker among the rock needles,
Squat and suck the dry juice, inspect
The eggs of shadow beneath the surface, twitching
Madly in their cells.
                    The earth, at the full,
Hangs in blue splendour in the sky.
                              I believe I have heard
Of this place.
                    In the mind darkness tosses:
The light deceives. A vivid ghost sea
Quivers and dazzles for miles.
                              Let us take the waters.
Stoop down, run the fingers along the brink.
It has a human taste, but sterile; odourless.
Massed human wills...
                         A dust plain flickering...
I think this is the Sea of Disappointment.

HEN WOMAN

The noon heat in the yard
smelled of stillness and coming thunder.
A hen scratched and picked at the shore.
It stopped, its body crouched and puffed out.
The brooding silence seemed to say 'Hush...'

The cottage door opened,
a black hole
in a whitewashed wall so bright
the eyes narrowed.
Inside, a clock murmured 'Gong...'

(I had felt all this before...)

She hurried out in her slippers
muttering, her face dark with anger,
and gathered the hen up jerking
languidly. Her hand fumbled.
Too late. Too late.

It fixed me with its pebble eyes
(seeing what mad blur?).
A white egg showed in the sphincter;
mouth and beak opened together;
and time stood still.

Nothing moved: bird or woman,
fumbled or fumbling – locked there
(as I must have been) gaping.

*

There was a tiny movement at my feet,
tiny and mechanical; I looked down.
A beetle like a bronze leaf
was inching across the cement,
clasping with small tarsi
a ball of dung bigger than its body.
The serrated brow pressed the ground humbly,
lifted in a short stare, bowed again;
the dung-ball advanced minutely,
losing a few fragments,
specks of staleness and freshness.

*

A mutter of thunder far off
– time not quite stopped.
I saw the egg had moved a fraction:
a tender blank brain
under torsion, a clean new world.

As I watched, the mystery completed.
The black zero of the orifice
closed to a point
and the white zero of the egg hung free,
flecked with greenish brown oils.

It slowly turned and fell.
Dreamlike, fussed by her splayed fingers,
it floated outward, moon-white,
leaving no trace in the air,
and began its drop to the shore.

                    *

I feed upon it still, as you see;
there is no end to that which,
not understood, may yet be noted
and hoarded in the imagination,
in the yolk of one's being, so to speak,
there to undergo its (quite animal) growth,
dividing blindly,
twitching, packed with will,
searching in its own tissue
for the structure
in which it may wake.
Something that had — clenched
in its cave — not been
now was: an egg of being.
Through what seemed a whole year it fell
— as it still falls, for me,
solid and light, the red gold beating
in its silvery womb,
alive as the yolk and white
of my eye; as it will continue
to fall, probably until I die,
through the vast indifferent spaces
with which I am empty.

                    *

It smashed against the grating
and slipped down quickly out of sight.
It was over in a comical flash.
The soft mucous shell clung a little longer,
then drained down.

She stood staring, in blank anger.
Then her eyes came to life, and she laughed
and let the bird flap away.
'It's all the one.
There's plenty more where that came from!'

Hen to pan!
It was a simple world.

TEAR

I was sent in to see her.
A fringe of jet drops
chattered at my ear
as I went in through the hangings.

I was swallowed in chambery dusk.
My heart shrank
at the smell of disused
organs and sour kidney.

The black aprons I used to
bury my face in
were folded at the foot of the bed
in the last watery light from the window

(Go in and say goodbye to her)
and I was carried off
to unfathomable depths.
I turned to look at her.

She stared at the ceiling
and puffed her cheek, distracted,
propped high in the bed
resting for the next attack.

The covers were gathered close
up to her mouth,
that the lines of ill-temper still
marked. Her grey hair

was loosened out like
a young woman's all over
the pillow, mixed with the shadows
criss-crossing her forehead

and at her mouth and eyes,
like a web of strands tying down her head
and tangling down toward the shadow
eating away the floor at my feet.

I couldn't stir at first, nor wished to,
for fear she might turn and tempt me
(my own father's mother)
with open mouth

— with some fierce wheedling whisper —
to hide myself one last time
against her, and bury my
self in her drying mud.

Was I to kiss her? As soon
kiss the damp that crept
in the flowered walls
of this pit.

Yet I had to kiss.
I knelt by the bulk of the death bed
and sank my face in the chill
and smell of her black aprons.

Snuff and musk, the folds against my eyelids,
carried me into a derelict place
smelling of ash: unseen walls and roofs
rustled like breathing.

I found myself disturbing
dead ashes for any trace
of warmth, when far off
in the vaults a single drop

splashed. And I found
what I was looking for
— not heat nor fire,
not any comfort,

but her voice, soft, talking to someone
about my father: 'God help him, he cried
big tears over there by the machine
for the poor little thing.' Bright

drops on the wooden lid for
my infant sister. My own
wail of child-animal grief
was soon done, with any early guess

at sad dullness and tedious pain
and lives bitter with hard bondage.
How I tasted it now —
her heart beating in my mouth!

She drew an uncertain breath
and pushed at the clothes
and shuddered tiredly.
I broke free

and left the room
promising myself
when she was really dead
I would really kiss.

My grandfather half looked up
from the fireplace as I came out,
and shrugged and turned back
with a deaf stare to the heat.

I fidgeted beside him for a minute
and went out to the shop.
It was still bright there
and I felt better able to breathe.

Old age can digest
anything: the commotion
at Heaven's gate — the struggle
in store for you all your life.

How long and hard it is
before you get to Heaven,
unless like little Agnes
you vanish with early tears.

SACRIFICE

Crowded steps, a sea of white faces
streaked with toil.

The scrutiny is over, in sunlight,
terrible black and white.

There is the mark... In those streaks...
Their hands are on her.
Her friends gather.
The multitudes sigh and bless
and persuade her heavily forward to her tears
in doomed excitement
down the cup of light
and onto her back on the washed bricks
with breasts held apart
and midriff fluttering in the sun.

The souls gather unseen, like wisps of hunger,
hovering above the table, not interfering,
as it is done in a shivering flash.
The vivid pale solid of the breast
dissolves in a crimson flood.
The heart flops in its sty.

                              *

Never mind the hurt. I've never felt
so terribly alive, so ready, so gripped
by love — gloved fingers slippery
next the heart!

                    Is it very difficult?

The blinding pain — when love goes direct
and wrenches at the heart-strings! But the pangs
quickly pass their maximum, and then
such a fount of tenderness!

                              Are you stuck?

Let me arch back.

                    I love how you keep muttering

'You know now...' — and your concern...
but you must finish it.
I lose my mind gladly, thinking:
the heart — in another's clutches!

We are each other's knowledge. It is peace that
                                              counts,
and knowledge brings peace, even thrust crackling
into the skull and bursting with tongues of fire.
Peace. Love dying down, as love ascends.

I love your tender triumph, straightening up,
lifting your reddened sleeves. The stain spreads
                                    downward
through your great flushed pinions.
You are a real angel.
My heart is in your hands: mind it well.

CRAB ORCHARD SANCTUARY: LATE OCTOBER

The lake water lifted a little and fell
doped and dreamy in the late heat.
The air at lung temperature — like the end of the world:
a butterfly panted with dull scarlet wings
on the mud by the reeds, the tracks
of small animals softening along the edge,
a child's foot-prints, out too far...

The car park was empty. Long threads of spider silk
blew out softly from the tips of the trees.
A big spider stopped on the warm gravel,
sunlight charging the dark shell.

A naked Indian stepped out onto the grass
silent and savage, faded,
grew transparent, disappeared.

A speedboat glistened slowly in the distance.
A column of smoke climbed from the opposite shore.
In the far inlets clouds of geese flew about
quarreling and settling in.

*

                                    That morning
two thin quails appeared in our garden
stepping one by one with piping movements
across the grass, feeding. I watched a long time
until they rounded the corner of the house.
A few grey wasps still floated about at the eaves;
crickets still chirruped in the grass
— but in growing silence — after last week's frosts.
Now a few vacated bodies, locust wraiths,
light as dry scale, begin to drift
on the driveway among the leaves,
stiff little Fuseli devil bodies.
Hidden everywhere, a myriad
leather seed-cases lie in wait
nourishing curled worms of white fat
— ugly, in absolute certainty, piteous,
threatening in every rustling sound:
bushes worrying in the night breeze,
dry leaves detaching, and creeping.
They will swarm again, on suffocated nights,
with their endless hysterics; and wither away again.

                    *

Who will stand still then, listening
to that woodpecker knocking, and watch
the erratic jays and cardinals flashing
blue and red among the branches and trunks;
that bronze phantom pausing; and this... stock-still,
with glittering brain, withering away.

It is an ending already.
The road hot and empty, taken over
by spiders, and pairs of butterflies twirling
about one another, and grasshoppers leap-
drifting over the gravel, birds darting
fluttering through the heat.
                            What solitary step.

A slow hot glare out on the lake
spreading over the water.

FINISTÉRE

I...
One...

I smelt the weird Atlantic.
Finistére...
Finistére...

The sea surface darkened. The land behind me,
and all its cells and cysts, grew dark.
From a bald boulder on the cairn top
I spied out the horizon to the northwest
and sensed that minute imperfection again.
Where the last sunken ray withdrew...
A point of light?

A maggot of the possible
wriggled out of the spine
into the brain.

We hesitated before that wider sea
but our heads sang with purpose
and predatory peace.
And whose excited blood was that
fumbling our movements? Whose ghostly hunger
tunneling our thoughts full of passages
smelling of death ash and clay and faint metals
and great stones in the darkness?

At no great distance out in the bay
the swell took us into its mercy,
grey upheaving slopes of water
Sliding under us, collapsing,
crawling onward, mountainous.

Driven outward a day and a night
we held fast, numbed by the steady
might of the oceanic wind.
We drew close together, as one,
and turned inward, salt chaos
rolling in silence all around us,
and listened to our own mouths
mumbling in the sting of spray:

—Ill wind end well
mild mother
on wild water pour peace

who gave us our unrest
whom we meet and unmeet
in whose yearning shadow
we erect our great uprights
and settle fulfilled
and build and are still
unsettled, whose goggle gaze
and holy howl we have scraped
speechless on slabs of stone
poolspirals opening on
closing spiralpools
and dances drilled in the rock
in coil zigzag angle and curl
river ripple earth ramp
suncircle moonloop...
in whose outflung service
we nourished our hunger
uprooted and came

in whale hell

                    gale gullet

salt hole

                    dark nowhere

calm queen

                    pour peace

The bad dream ended at last.
In the morning, in a sunny breeze,
bare headlands rose fresh out of the waves.
We entered a deep bay, lying open
to all the currents of the ocean.
We were further than anyone had ever been
and light-headed with exhaustion and relief
— three times we misjudged and were nearly driven
on the same rock.
                    (I had felt all this before...)

We steered in along a wall of mountain
and entered a quiet hall of rock echoing
to the wave-wash and our low voices.
I stood at the prow. We edged to a slope of stone.
I steadied myself. 'Our Father...', someone said
and there was a little laughter. I stood
searching a moment for the right words.
They fell silent. I chose the old words once more
and stepped out. At the solid shock
a dreamy power loosened at the base of my spine
and uncoiled and slid up through the marrow.
A flow of seawater over the rock fell back
with a she-hiss, plucking at my heel.
My tongue stumbled

Who
      is a breath
that makes the wind
that makes the wave
that makes   this   voice?

Who
      is the bull with seven scars
the hawk on the cliff
the salmon sunk in his pool
the pool sunk in her soil
the animal's fury
the flower's fibre
a teardrop in the sun?

Who
      is the word that spoken
the spear springs
      and pours out terror
the spark springs
      and burns in the brain?

When men meet on the hill
dumb as stones in the dark
      (the craft knocked behind me)
who is the jack of all light?
Who goes in full into
the moon's interesting conditions?
Who fingers the sun's sink hole?
      (I went forward, reaching out)

A TECHNICAL SUPPLEMENT

IV
The point, greatly enlarged,
pushed against the skin
depressing an area of tissue.
Rupture occurred: at first a separation
at the intensest place among the cells
then a deepening damage
with nerve-strings fraying
and snapping and writhing back.
Blood welled up to fill the wound,
bathing the point as it went deeper.

Persist.
        Beyond a certain depth
it stands upright by itself
and quivers with borrowed life.

Persist.
        And you may find
the buried well. And take on
the stillness of a root.

Quietus.

              Or:

V
A blade licks out and acts
with one tongue.
Jets of blood respond
in diverse tongues.

And promptly.
A single sufficient cut
and the body drops at once.
No reserve. Inert.

If you would care to enter this grove of beasts:

VI
A veteran smiled and let us pass through
to the dripping groves in Swift's slaughterhouse,
hot confusion and the scream-rasp of the saw.
Huge horned fruit not quite dead
— chained, hooked by one hock, stunned
above a pool of steaming spiceblood.

Two elderly men in aprons waded back and forth
with long knives they sharpened slowly and
inserted, tapping cascades of black blood
that collapsed before their faces onto the concrete.
Another fallen beast landed, kicking,
and was hooked by the ankle and hoisted into its place.

They come in behind a plank barrier on an upper level
walking with erect tail to the stunning place...
Later in the process they encounter
a man who loosens the skin around their tails
with deep cuts in unexpected directions;
The tail springs back; the hide pulls down to the jaws.

With the sheep it was even clearer
they were dangling alive, the blood trickling
over nostrils and teeth. A flock of them waited their turn
crowded into the furthest corner of the pen,
some looking back over their shoulders
at us, in our window.

Great bulks of pigs hung from dainty heels,
the full sow-throats cut open the wrong way.
Three negroes stood on a raised bench before them.
One knifed the belly open upward to the tail
until the knife and his hands disappeared
in the fleshy vulva and broke some bone.

The next opened it downward to the throat,
embraced the mass of entrails, lifted them out
and dropped them in a chute. And so to one
who excavated the skull through flaps of the face,
hooked it onto the carcase and pushed all forward
toward a frame of blue flames, the singeing machine.

At a certain point it is all merely meat,
sections hung or stacked in a certain order.
Downstairs a row of steel barrows
holds the liquid heaps of organs.
As each new piece drops, adding itself,
the contents tremble throughout their mass.

In a clean room a white-coated worker
positioned a ham, found a blood vessel with a forceps,
clipped it to a tube of red chemical
and pumped the piece full. It swelled immediately
and saturated: tiny crimson jets
poured from it everywhere. Transfused!

C. G. JUNG'S 'FIRST YEARS'

I

Dark waters churn amongst us
and whiten against troublesome obstacles:

A nurse's intimate warm ear
far in the past; the sallow loin of her throat;
and more — her song at twilight
as she dreamily (let us now suppose)
combined in her entrails
memories of womanly manipulations
with further detailed plans for the living flesh.

II

Jesus, and his graves eating the dead...
A Jesuit — a witchbat —
toiled with outspread sleeves down
the path from a wooded hilltop...
A pillar of skin
stared up dumb, enthroned
in an underground room...

The dreams broke in succession and ran back
whispering with disappearing particulars.

*

Since when I have eaten Jesus...
and stepped onto the path
        long ago: my fingers stretched at the hill
        and a sleeve-winged terror
        shrank like a shadow and flapped away
        sailing over the dry grass;
        staring crumbs led up through the tree-darkness
        to a hollow, with bloody steps down...
and have assumed the throne.

JOHN MONTAGUE
(1929-)

WOODTOWN MANOR
for Morris Graves
I
Here the delicate dance of silence,
The quick step of the robin,
The sudden skittering rush of the wren:
Minute essences move in and out of creation
Until the skin of soundlessness forms again.

Part order, part wilderness,
Water creates its cadenced illusion
Of glaucous, fluent growth;
Fins raised, as in a waking dream,
Bright fish probe their painted stream.

Imaginary animals harbour here:
The young fox coiled in its covert,
Bright-eyed and mean, the baby bird:
The heron, like a tilted italic,
Illuminating the gospel of the absurd.

And all the menagerie of the living marvellous:
Stone shape of toad,
Flicker of insect life,
Shift of wind touched grass
As though a beneficent spirit stirred.

II
Twin deities hover in Irish air
Reconciling poles of east and west;
The detached and sensual Indian God,
Franciscan dream of gentleness:
Gravity of Georgian manor
Approves, with classic stare,
Their dual disciplines of tenderness.

A WELCOMING PARTY
Wie war das möglich?

That final newsreel of the war:
A welcoming party of almost shades
Met us at the cinema door
Clicking what remained of their heels.

From nests of bodies like hatching eggs
Flickered insectlike hands and legs
And rose an ululation, terrible, shy;
Children conjugating the verb 'to die'.

One clamoured mutely of love
From a mouth like a burnt glove;
Others upheld hands bleak as begging bowls
Claiming the small change of our souls.

Some smiled at us as protectors.
Can these bones live?
Our parochial brand of innocence
Was all we had to give.

To be always at the periphery of incident
Gave my childhood its Irish dimension; drama of unevent:
Yet doves of mercy, as doves of air,
Can falter here as anywhere.

That long dead Sunday in Armagh
I learned one meaning of total war
And went home to my Christian school
To kick a football through the air.

LIKE DOLMENS ROUND MY CHILDHOOD,
THE OLD PEOPLE

Like dolmens round my childhood, the old people.

Jamie MacCrystal sang to himself,
A broken song without tune, without words;
He tipped me a penny every pension day,
Fed kindly crusts to winter birds.
When he died, his cottage was robbed,
Mattress and money box torn and searched.
Only the corpse they didn't disturb.

Maggie Owens was surrounded by animals,
A mongrel bitch and shivering pups,
Even in her bedroom a she-goat cried.
She was a well of gossip defiled,
Fanged chronicler of a whole countryside:
Reputed a witch, all I could find
Was her lonely need to deride.

The Nialls lived along a mountain lane
Where heather bells bloomed, clumps of foxglove.
All were blind, with Blind Pension and Wireless,
Dead eyes serpent-flicked as one entered
To shelter from a downpour of mountain rain.
Crickets chirped under the rocking hearthstone
Until the muddy sun shone out again.

Mary Moore lived in a crumbling gatehouse,
Famous as Pisa for its leaning gable.
Bag-apron and boots, she tramped the fields
Driving lean cattle from a miry stable.
A by-word for fierceness, she fell asleep
Over love stories, Red Star and Red Circle,
Dreamed of gypsy love rites, by firelight sealed.

Wild Billy Eagleson married a Catholic servant girl
When all his Loyal family passed on:
We danced round him shouting 'To Hell with King Billy',
And dodged from the arc of his flailing blackthorn.
Forsaken by both creeds, he showed little concern
Until the Orange drums banged past in the summer
And bowler and sash aggressively shone.

Curate and doctor trudged to attend them,
Through knee-deep snow, through summer heat,
From main road to lane to broken path,
Gulping the mountain air with painful breath.
Sometimes they were found by neighbours,
Silent keepers of a smokeless hearth,
Suddenly cast in the mould of death.

Ancient Ireland, indeed! I was reared by her bedside,
The rune and the chant, evil eye and averted head,
Fomorian fierceness of family and local feud.
Gaunt figures of fear and of friendliness,
For years they trespassed on my dreams,
Until once, in a standing circle of stones,
I felt their shadows pass

Into that dark permanence of ancient forms.

THE TROUT

Flat on the bank I parted
Rushes to ease my hands
In the water without a ripple
And tilt them slowly downstream
To where he lay, light as a leaf,
In his fluid sensual dream.

Bodiless lord of creation
I hung briefly above him
Savouring my own absence
Senses expanding in the slow
Motion, the photographic calm
That grows before action.

As the curve of my hands
Swung under his body
He surged, with visible pleasure.
I was so preternaturally close
I could count every stipple
But still cast no shadow, until

The two palms crossed in a cage
Under the lightly pulsing gills.
Then (entering my own enlarged
Shape, which rode on the water)
I gripped. To this day I can
Taste his terror on my hands.

ALL LEGENDARY OBSTACLES

All legendary obstacles lay between
Us, the long imaginary plain,
The monstrous ruck of mountains
And, swinging across the night,
Flooding the Sacramento, San Joaquin,
The hissing drift of winter rain.

All day I waited, shifting
Nervously from station to bar
As I saw another train sail
By, the San Francisco Chief or
Golden Gate, water dripping
From great flanged wheels.

At midnight you came, pale
Above the negro porter's lamp.
I was too blind with rain
And doubt to speak, but
Reached from the platform
Until our chilled hands met.

You had been travelling for days
With an old lady, who marked
A neat circle on the glass
With her glove, to watch us
Move into the wet darkness
Kissing, still unable to speak.

A CHOSEN LIGHT

I *Il rue Daguerre*
At night, sometimes, when I cannot sleep
I go to the *atelier* door
And smell the earth of the garden.

It exhales softly,
Especially now, approaching springtime,
When tendrils of green are plaited

Across the humus, desperately frail
In their passage against
The dark, unredeemed parcels of earth.

There is white light on the cobblestones
And in the apartment house opposite —
All four floors — silence.

In that stillness — soft but luminously exact,
A chosen light — I notice that
The tips of the lately grafted cherry-tree

Are a firm and lacquered black.

II *Salute, in passing*
The voyagers we cannot follow
Are the most haunting. That face
Time has worn to a fastidious mask
Chides me, as one strict master
Steps through the Luxembourg.
Surrounded by children, lovers,
His thoughts are rigorous as trees
Reduced by winter. While the water
Parts for tiny white-rigged yachts
He plots an icy human mathematics —
Proving what content sighs when all
Is lost, what wit flares from nothingness:
His handsome hawk head is sacrificial
As he weathers to how man now is.

III *Radiometers in the rue Jacob*
In the twin
Or triple crystalline spheres
The tiny fans of mica flash;
Snow fleeing on dark ground.

I imagine
One on an executive's desk
Whirling above the memoranda
Or by his mistress's bed

(next to the milk-white telephone)

A minute wind-
Mill casting its pale light
Over unhappiness, ceaselessly
Elaborating its signals

Not of help, but of neutral energy

SUMMER STORM

I   *A Door Banging*

Downstairs, a door
banging, like a
blow upon sleep

pain bleeding
away in gouts
of accusation &

counter accusation:
heart's release
of bitter speech.

II   *Mosquito Hunt*

Heat contracts the
walls, smeared with
the bodies of insects

we crush, absurd-
ly balanced on the
springs of the bed

twin shadows on
the wall rising
& falling as

we swoop &
quarrel, like
wide winged bats.

III   *Tides*

The window blown
open, that summer
night, a full moon

occupying the sky
with a pressure of
underwater light

old virgin, which he rummages while
she battles for life
                    bony fingers
reaching desperately to push
against his bull neck. 'I prayed
to the Blessed Virgin herself
for help and after a time
I broke his grip.'
                    He rolls
to the floor, snores asleep,
while she cowers until dawn
and the dogs' whimpering starts
him awake, to lurch back across
the wet bog.

III
                    And still
the dog rose shines in the hedge.
Petals beaten wide by rain, it
sways slightly, at the tip of a
slender, tangled, arching branch
which, with her stick, she gathers
into us.
              'The wild rose
is the only rose without thorns',
she says, holding a wet blossom
for a second, in a hand knotted
as the knob of her stick.
'Whenever I see it, I remember
the Holy Mother of God and
all she suffered.'
                    Briefly
the air is strong with the smell
of that weak flower, offering
its crumbled yellow cup
and pale bleeding lips
fading to white
                    at the rim
of each bruised and heart-
shaped petal.

SPECIAL DELIVERY

The spider's web
of your handwriting
on a blue envelope

brings up too much
to bear, old sea-sick-
ness of love, retch

of sentiment, night
& day devoured by
the worm of delight

which turns to
feed upon itself;
emotion running so

wildly to seed
between us that
it assumes a third,

a ghost or child's
face, the soft skull
pale as an eggshell

& the life-cord
of the emerging body —
fish, reptile, bird —

which trails
like the cable
of an astronaut

as we whirl & turn
in our bubble of
blood & sperm

before the gravities
of earth claim us
from limitless space.

Now, light years later
your nostalgic letter
admitting failure,

claiming forgiveness.
When fire pales to
so faint an ash

so frail a design
why measure guilt
your fault or mine:

but blood seeps where
I sign before tearing
down the perforated line.

*

orge Hill:
*Historical
count of the
antation of
ster*

And who ever heard
Such a sight unsung
As a severed head
With a grafted tongue?
Old Rhyme

ir Thomas Phillips made a journey
rom Coleraine to Dungannon, through
he wooded country... and thereupon
vrote to Salisbury, expressing... his
unfeigned astonishment at the sight of
o many cattle and such abundance of
rain... The hillsides were literally
overed with cattle... the valleys were
lothed in the rich garniture of ripening
arley and oats; while the woods
warmed with swine... 20,000 of these
eing easily fattened yearly in the
orest of Glenconkeyne alone.

Our geographers do not forget
what entertainment the Irish of
Tyrone gave to a mapmaker
about the end of the late rebellion;
or one Barkeley being appointed
by the late Earl of Devonshire to
draw a true and perfect map of
he north part of Ulster... when
ie came into Tyrone the inhabi-
ants took off his head...
Sir John Davies

A SEVERED HEAD

I   *The Road's End*

May, and the air is light
On eye, on hand. As I take
The mountain road, my former step
Doubles mine, driving cattle
To the upland fields. Between
Shelving ditches of whitethorn
They sway their burdensome
Bodies, tempted at each turn
By hollows of sweet grass,
Pale clover, while memory,
A restive sally switch, flicks
Across their backs.
           The well
Is still there, a half-way mark
Between two cottages, opposite
The gate in Danaghy's field,
But above the protective dry-
Stone rim, the plaiting thorns
Have not been bill-hooked back
And a thick *glaur* floats.
No need to rush to head off
The cattle from sinking soft
Muzzles into leaf smelling
Spring water.
           From the farm
Nearby, I hear a yard tap gush
And a collie bark, to check
My presence. Our farmhands
Lived there, wife and children
In twin white-washed cells,
An iron roof burning in summer.
Now there is a kitchen extension
With radio aerial, rough outhouses
For coal and tractor. A housewife
Smiles good-day as I step through
The fluff and dust of her walled
Farmyard, solicited by raw-necked
Stalking turkeys
     to where cart
Ruts shape the ridge of a valley,

One of many among the switch-
Back hills of what old chroniclers
Called the Star Bog. Uncurling
Fern, white scut of *canavan,*
Spars of bleached bog fir jutting
From heather, make a landscape
So light in wash it must be learnt
Day after day, in shifting detail,
Out to the pale Sperrins.
'I like to look across', said
Barney Horisk, leaning on his *slean,*
'and think of all the people
Who have bin'.
                Like shards
Of a lost culture, the slopes
Are strewn with cabins, deserted
In my lifetime. Here the older
People sheltered; the Blind Nialls,
Big Ellen, who had been a Fair-
Day prostitute. The bushes cramp
To the evening wind as I reach
The road's end. Jamie MacCrystal
Lived in the final cottage,
A trim grove of mountain ash
Soughed protection round his walls
And bright painted gate. The thatch
Has slumped in, white dust of nettles
On the flags. Only the shed remains
In use for calves, although fuschia
Bleeds by the wall, and someone has
Propped a yellow cartwheel
Against the door.

THE LEAPING FIRE
I. M. Brigid Montague (1876-1966)

A MIRACLE
Each morning, from the corner
Of the hearth, I saw a miracle
as you sifted the smoored ashes
to blow
             a fire's sleeping remains
back to life, holding the burning brands
of turf, between work hardened hands.
I draw on that fire...

The Little Flower's
              Disciple

I
Old lady, I now celebrate
to whom I owe so much;
bending over me in darkness
a scaly tenderness of touch

skin of bony arm & elbow
sandpapered with work:
because things be to be done
and simplicity did not shirk

the helpless, hopeless task
of maintaining a family farm,
which meant, by legal fiction,
maintaining a family name.

The thongless man's boots,
the shapeless bag apron:
would your favourite saint
accept the harness of humiliation

you bore constantly until
the hiss of milk into the pail
became as lonely a prayer as
your vigil at the altar rail.

Roses showering from heaven
upon Her uncorrupted body
after death, celebrated
the Little Flower's sanctity

& through the latticed grill
of your patron's enclosed order
an old French nun once threw me
a tiny sack of lavender.

So from the pressed herbs
of your least memory, sweetness exudes:
that of the meek and the selfless,
who should be comforted.

2

The Living & the
Dead

Nightly she climbs the
narrow length of the stairs
to kneel in her cold room
as if she would storm
heaven with her prayers —

which, if they have power,
now reach across the quiet
night of death to where
instead of a worn rosary,
I tell these metal keys.

The pain of a whole family
she gathers into her hands:
the pale mother who died
to give birth to children
scattered to the four winds

who now creakingly arouse
from darkness, distance
to populate the corners
of this silent house
they once knew so well.

A draught whipped candle
magnifies her shadow —
a frail body grown monstrous,
sighing in a trance
before the gilt crucifix —

& as the light gutters
the shadows gather to dance
on the wall of the next room
where, a schoolboy searching sleep,
I begin to touch myself.

The sap of another generation
fingering through a broken tree
to push fresh branches
towards a further light,
a different identity.

Omagh
hospital

3
Your white hair
on the thin rack
of your shoulders

it is hard to
look into the eyes
of the dying

who carry away
a part of oneself —
a shared world

& you, whose life
was selflessness,
now die slowly

broken down by
process to a pale
exhausted beauty

the moon in her
last phase, caring
only for herself.

I lean over the
bed, but you barely
recognize me &

when an image
forces entry —
Is that John?

Bring me home
you whimper &
I see a house

Shaken by traffic
until a fault runs
from roof to base

but your face has
already retired into
the blind, animal

misery of age
paying out your
rosary beads

hands twitching
as you drift
towards nothingness.

4
Family legend held
that this frail
woman had heard
the banshee's wail

& on the night
she lay dying
I heard a low,
constant crying

over the indifferent
roofs of Paris —
the marsh bittern
or white owl sailing

from its foul
nest of bones
to warn me with
a hollow note

& among autobuses
& taxis, the shrill
paraphernalia of a
swollen city

I crossed myself
from rusty habit
before I realise
why I had done it.

A hollow note.

COURTYARD IN WINTER

Snow curls in on the cold wind.

Slowly, I push back the door.
After long absence, old habits
Are painfully revived, those disciplines
Which enable us to survive,
To keep a minimal fury alive
While flake by faltering flake

Snow curls in on the cold wind.

Along the courtyard, the boss
Of each cobblestone is rimmed
In white, with winter's weight
Pressing, like a silver shield.
On all the small plots of earth,
Inert in their living death as

Snow curls in on the cold wind.

Seized in a giant fist of frost,
The grounded planes at London Airport,
Mallarme swans, trapped in ice.
The friend whom I have just left
Will be dead, a year from now
Through her own fault, while

Snow curls in on the cold wind.

Or smothered by some glacial truth?
Thirty years ago, I learnt to reach
Across the rusting hoops of steel
That bound our greening waterbarrel
To save the living water beneath
The hardening crust of ice, before

Snow curls in on the cold wind.

But despair has a deeper crust.
In all our hours together, I never
Managed to ease the single hurt
That edged her towards her death;

Never reached through her loneliness
To save a trust, chilled after

Snow curls in on the cold wind.

I plunged through snowdrifts once,
Above our home, to carry
A telegram to a mountain farm.
Fearful but inviting, they waved me
To warm myself at the flaring
Hearth before I faced again where

Snow curls in on the cold wind.

The news I brought was sadness.
In a far city, someone of their name
Lay dying. The tracks of foxes,
Wild birds as I climbed down
Seemed to form a secret writing
Minute and frail as life when

Snow curls in on the cold wind.

Sometimes, I know that message.
There is a disease called snow-sickness;
The glare from the bright god,
The earth's reply. As if that
Ceaseless, glittering light was
All the truth we'd left after

Snow curls in on the cold wind.

So, before dawn, comfort fails.
I imagine her end, in some sad
Bedsitting room, the steady hiss
Of the gas more welcome than an
Act of friendship, the protective
Oblivion of a lover's caress if

Snow curls in on the cold wind.

In the canyon of the street
The dark snowclouds hesitate,
Turning to slush almost before

They cross the taut canvas of
The street stalls, the bustle
Of a sweeper's brush after

Snow curls in on the cold wind.

The walls are spectral, white.
All the trees black-ribbed, bare.
Only veins of ivy, the sturdy
Laurel with its waxen leaves,
Its scant red berries, survive
To form a winter wreath as

Snow curls in on the cold wind.

*

What solace but endurance, kindness?
Against her choice, I still affirm
That nothing dies, that even from
Such bitter failure memory grows;
The snowflake's structure, fragile
But intricate as the rose when

Snow curls in on the cold wind.

DOWAGER

I dwell in this leaky Western castle.
American matrons weave across the carpet,
Sorefooted as camels, and less useful.

Smooth Ionic columns hold up a roof.
A chandelier shines on a foxhound's coat:
The grandson of a grandmother I reared.

In the old days I read or embroidered,
But now it is enough to see the sky change,
Clouds extend or smother a mountain's shape.

Wet afternoons I ride in the Rolls;
Windshield wipers flail helpless against the rain:
I thrash through pools like smashing panes of glass.

And the light afterwards! Hedges steam,
I ride through a damp tunnel of sweetness,
The bonnet strewn with bridal hawthorn

From which a silver lady leaps, always young.
Alone, I hum with satisfaction in the sun,
An old bitch, with a warm mouthful of game.

A GRAVEYARD IN QUEENS
for Eileen Carney

We hesitate along
flower encumbered

avenues of the dead;
Greek, Puerto-Rican,.

Italian, Irish —
(our true Catholic

world, a graveyard)
but a squirrel

dances us to it
through the water

sprinklered grass,
collapsing wreaths,

& taller than you
by half, lately from

that hidden village
where you were born

I sway with you
in a sad, awkward

dance of pain
over the grave of

my uncle & namesake —
the country fiddler —

& the grave of almost
all your life held,

your husband & son
all three sheltering

under the same
squat, grey stone.

                    *

You would cry out
against what has

happened, such
heedless hurt,

had you the harsh
nature for it

(swelling the North
wind with groans,

curses, imprecations
against heaven's will)

but your mind is
a humble house, a

soft light burning
beneath the holy

picture, the image
of the seven times

wounded heart of
her, whose portion

is to endure. For
there is no end

to pain, nor of
love to match it

& I remember Anne
meekest of my aunts

rocking & praying
in her empty room.

Oh, the absurdity
of grief in that

doll's house, all
the chair legs sawn

to nurse dead children:
love's museum!

*

It sent me down
to the millstream

to spy upon a
mournful waterhen

shushing her young
along the autumn

flood, as seriously
as a policeman and

after scampering
along, the proud

plumed squirrel
now halts, to stand

at the border
of this grave plot

serious, still,
a small ornament

holding something
a nut, a leaf —

like an offering
inside its paws.

*

For an instant
you smile to see

his antics, then
bend to tidy

flowers, gravel
like any woman

making a bed,
arranging a room,

over what were
your darlings' heads

and far from
our supposed home

I submit again
to stare soberly

at my own name
cut on a gravestone

& hear the creak
of a ghostly fiddle

filter through
American earth

the slow pride
of a lament.

HERBERT STREET REVISITED
for Madeleine

I
A light is burning late
in this Georgian Dublin street:
someone is leading our old lives!

And our black cat scampers again
through the wet grass of the convent garden
upon his masculine errands.

The pubs shut: a released bull,
Behan shoulders up the street,
topples into our basement, roaring 'John!'

A pony and donkey cropped flank
by flank under the trees opposite;
short neck up, long neck down,

as Nurse Mullen knelt by her bedside
to pray for her lost Mayo hills,
the bruised bodies of Easter Volunteers.

Animals, neighbours, treading the pattern
of one time and place into history,
like our early marriage, while

tall windows looked down upon us
from walls flushed light pink or salmon
watching and enduring succession.

II
As I leave, you whisper,
'don't betray our truth'
and like a ghost dancer,
invoking a lost tribal strength
I halt in tree-fed darkness

to summon back our past,
and celebrate a love that eased
so kindly, the dying bone,
enabling the spirit to sing
of old happiness, when alone.

III
So put the leaves back on the tree,
put the tree back in the ground,
let Brendan trundle his corpse down
the street singing, like Molly Malone.

Let the black cat, tiny emissary
of our happiness, streak again
through the darkness, to fall soft
clawed into a landlord's dustbin.

Let Nurse Mullen take the last
train to Westport, and die upright
in her chair, facing a window
warm with the blue slopes of Nephin.

And let the pony and donkey come —
look, someone has left the gate open —
like hobbyhorses linked in
the slow motion of a dream

parading side by side, down
the length of Herbert Street,
rising and falling, lifting
their hooves through the moonlight.

THE POINT

Rocks jagged in morning mist.
At intervals, the foghorn sounds
From the white lighthouse rock
Lonely as cow mourning her calf,
Groaning, belly deep, desperate.

I assisted at such failure once;
A night-long fight to save a calf
Born finally, with broken neck.
It flailed briefly on the straw,
A wide-eyed mother straddling it.

Listen carefully. This is different.
It sounds to guide, not lament.

When the defining light is powerless,
Ships hesitating down the strait
Hear its harsh voice as friendliness.

Upstairs my wife & daughter sleep.
Our two lives have separated now
But I would send my voice to yours
Cutting through the shrouding mist
Like some friendly signal in distress.

The fog is lifting, slowly.
Flag high, a new ship is entering.
The opposite shore unveils itself,
Bright in detail as a painting,
Alone, but equal to the morning.

EDGE

Edenlike as your name
this sea's edge garden
where we rest, beneath
the clarity of a lighthouse.

To fly into risk,
attempt the dream,
cast off, as we have done,
requires true luck

who know ourselves
blessed to have found
between this harbour's arms
a sheltering home

where the vast tides of the Atlantic
lift to caress
rose coloured rocks.

So fate relents.
Hushed and calm,
safe and secret,
on the edge is best.

S E A M U S   H E A N E Y
(1939-   )

SEAMUS HEANEY

DIGGING

Between my finger and my thumb
The squat pen rests; snug as a gun.

Under my window, a clean rasping sound
When the spade sinks into gravelly ground:
My father, digging. I look down

Till his straining rump among the flowerbeds
Bends low, comes up twenty years away
Stooping in rhythm through potato drills
Where he was digging.

The coarse boot nestled on the lug, the shaft
Against the inside knee was levered firmly.
He rooted out tall tops, buried the bright edge deep
To scatter new potatoes that we picked
Loving their cool hardness in our hands.

By God, the old man could handle a spade.
Just like his old man.

My grandfather cut more turf in a day
Than any other man on Toner's bog.
Once I carried him milk in a bottle
Corked sloppily with paper. He straightened up
To drink it, then fell to right away

Nicking and slicing neatly, heaving sods
Over his shoulder, going down and down
For the good turf. Digging.

The cold smell of potato mould, the squelch and slap
Of soggy peat, the curt cuts of an edge
Through living roots awaken in my head.
But I've no spade to follow men like them.

Between my finger and my thumb
The squat pen rests.
I'll dig with it.

FOLLOWER

My father worked with a horse-plough,
His shoulders globed like a full sail strung
Between the shafts and the furrow.
The horses strained at his clicking tongue.

An expert. He would set the wing
And fit the bright steel-pointed sock.
The sod rolled over without breaking.
At the headrig, with a single pluck

Of reins, the sweating team turned round
And back into the land. His eye
Narrowed and angled at the ground,
Mapping the furrow exactly.

I stumbled in his hob-nailed wake,
Fell sometimes on the polished sod;
Sometimes he rode me on his back
Dipping and rising to his plod.

I wanted to grow up and plough,
To close one eye, stiffen my arm.
All I ever did was follow
In his broad shadow round the farm.

I was a nuisance, tripping, falling,
Yapping always. But today
It is my father who keeps stumbling
Behind me, and will not go away.

AT A POTATO DIGGING

I
A mechanical digger wrecks the drill,
Spins up a dark shower of roots and mould.
Labourers swarm in behind, stoop to fill
Wicker creels. Fingers go dead in the cold.

Like crows attacking crow-black fields, they stretch
A higgledy line from hedge to headland;
Some pairs keep breaking ragged ranks to fetch
A full creel to the pit and straighten, stand

Tall for a moment but soon stumble back
To fish a new load from the crumbled surf.
Heads bow, trunks bend, hands fumble towards the black
Mother. Processional stooping through the turf

Recurs mindlessly as autumn. Centuries
Of fear and homage to the famine god
Toughen the muscles behind their humbled knees,
Make a seasonal altar of the sod.

II
Flint-white, purple. They lie scattered
like inflated pebbles. Native
to the black hutch of clay
where the halved seed shot and clotted
these knobbed and slit-eyed tubers seem
the petrified hearts of drills. Split
by the spade, they show white as cream.

Good smells exude from crumbled earth.
The rough bark of humus erupts
knots of potatoes (a clean birth)
whose solid feel, whose wet inside
promises taste of ground and root.
To be piled in pits; live skulls, blind-eyed.

III
Live skulls, blind-eyed, balanced on
wild higgledy skeletons
scoured the land in 'forty-five,
wolfed the blighted root and died.

The new potato, sound as stone,
putrefied when it had lain
three days in the long clay pit.
Millions rotted along with it.

Mouths tightened in, eyes died hard,
faces chilled to a plucked bird.
In a million wicker huts
beaks of famine snipped at guts.

A people hungering from birth,
grubbing, like plants, in the bitch earth,
were grafted with a great sorrow.
Hope rotted like a marrow.

Stinking potatoes fouled the land,
pits turned pus into filthy mounds:
and where potato diggers are
you still smell the running sore.

IV
Under a gay flotilla of gulls
The rhythm deadens, the workers stop.
Brown bread and tea in bright canfuls
Are served for lunch. Dead-beat, they flop

Down in the ditch and take their fill,
Thankfully breaking timeless fasts;
Then, stretched on the faithless ground, spill
Libations of cold tea, scatter crusts.

PERSONAL HELICON
For Michael Longley

As a child, they could not keep me from wells
And old pumps with buckets and windlasses.
I loved the dark drop, the trapped sky, the smells
Of waterweed, fungus and dank moss.

One, in a brickyard, with a rotted board top.
I savoured the rich crash when a bucket
Plummeted down at the end of a rope.
So deep you saw no reflection in it.

A shallow one under a dry stone ditch
Fructified like any aquarium.
When you dragged out long roots from the soft mulch
A white face hovered over the bottom.

Others had echoes, gave back your own call
With a clean new music in it. And one
Was scaresome for there, out of ferns and tall
Foxgloves, a rat slapped across my reflection.

Now, to pry into roots, to finger slime,
To stare big-eyed Narcissus, into some spring
Is beneath all adult dignity. I rhyme
To see myself, to set the darkness echoing.

THATCHER

Bespoke for weeks, he turned up some morning
Unexpectedly, his bicycle slung
With a light ladder and a bag of knives.
He eyed the old rigging, poked at the eaves,

Opened and handled sheaves of lashed wheat-straw.
Next, the bundled rods: hazel and willow
Were flicked for weight, twisted in case they'd snap.
It seemed he spent the morning warming up:

Then fixed the ladder, laid out well honed blades
And snipped at straw and sharpened ends of rods
That, bent in two, made a white-pronged staple
For pinning down his world, handful by handful.

Couchant for days on sods above the rafters
He shaved and flushed the butts, stitched all together
Into a sloped honeycomb, a stubble patch,
And left them gaping at his Midas touch.

THE WIFE'S TALE

When I had spread it all on linen cloth
Under the hedge, I called them over.
The hum and gulp of the thresher ran down
And the big belt slewed to a standstill, straw
Hanging undelivered in the jaws.
There was such quiet that I heard their boots
Crunching the stubble twenty yards away.

He lay down and said 'Give these fellows theirs.
I'm in no hurry,' plucking grass in handfuls
And tossing it in the air. 'That looks well.'
(He nodded at my white cloth on the grass.)
'I declare a woman could lay out a field
Though boys like us have little call for cloths.'
He winked, then watched me as I poured a cup
And buttered the thick slices that he likes.
'It's threshing better than I thought, and mind
It's good clean seed. Away over there and look.'
Always this inspection has to be made
Even when I don't know what to look for.

But I ran my hand in the half-filled bags
Hooked to the slots. It was hard as shot,
Innumerable and cool. The bags gaped
Where the chutes ran back to the stilled drum
And forks were stuck at angles in the ground
As javelins might mark lost battlefields.
I moved between them back across the stubble.

They lay in the ring of their own crusts and dregs
Smoking and saying nothing. 'There's good yield,
Isn't there?' — as proud as if he were the land itself —
'Enough for crushing and for sowing both.'
And that was it. I'd come and he had shown me
So I belonged no further to the work.
I gathered cups and folded up the cloth
And went. But they still kept their ease
Spread out, unbuttoned, grateful, under the trees.

BOGLAND
for T. P. Flanagan

We have no prairies
To slice a big sun at evening —
Everywhere the eye concedes to
Encroaching horizon,

Is wooed into the cyclops' eye
Of a tarn. Our unfenced country
Is bog that keeps crusting
Between the sights of the sun.

They've taken the skeleton
Of the Great Irish Elk
Out of the peat, set it up
An astounding crate full of air.

Butter sunk under
More than a hundred years
Was recovered salty and white.
The ground itself is kind, black butter

Melting and opening underfoot,
Missing its last definition
By millions of years.
They'll never dig coal here,

Only the waterlogged trunks
Of great firs, soft as pulp.
Our pioneers keep striking
Inwards and downwards,

Every layer they strip
Seems camped on before.
The bogholes might be Atlantic seepage.
The wet centre is bottomless.

GIFTS OF RAIN

I
Cloudburst and steady downpour now
for days.
        Still mammal,
straw-footed on the mud,
he begins to sense weather
by his skin.

A nimble snout of flood
licks over stepping stones
and goes uprooting.
           He fords
his life by sounding.
              Soundings.

II
A man wading lost fields
breaks the pane of flood:

a flower of mud-
water blooms up to his reflection

like a cut swaying
its red spoors through a basin.

His hands grub
where the spade has uncastled

sunken drills, an atlantis
he depends on. So

he is hooped to where he planted
and sky and ground

are running naturally among his arms
that grope the cropping land.

III
When rains were gathering
there would be an all-night
roaring off the ford.
Their world-schooled ear

could monitor the usual
confabulations, the race
slabbering past the gable,
the Moyola harping on

its gravel beds:
all spouts by daylight
brimmed with their own airs
and overflowed each barrel

in long tresses.
I cock my ear
at an absence —
in the shared calling of blood

arrives my need
for antediluvian lore.
Soft voices of the dead
are whispering by the shore

that I would question
(and for my children's sake)
about crops rotted, river mud
glazing the baked clay floor.

IV
The tawny guttural water
spells itself: Moyola
is its own score and consort,

bedding the locale
in the utterance,
reed music, an old chanter

breathing its mists
through vowels and history.
A swollen river,

a mating call of sound
rises to pleasure me, Dives,
hoarder of common ground.

THE TOLLUND MAN

I

Some day I will go to Aarhus
To see his peat-brown head,
The mild pods of his eye-lids,
His pointed skin cap.

In the flat country nearby
Where they dug him out,
His last gruel of winter seeds
Caked in his stomach,

Naked except for
The cap, noose and girdle,
I will stand for a long time.
Bridegroom to the goddess,

She tightened her torc on him
And opened her fen,
Those dark juices working
Him to a saint's kept body,

Trove of the turf-cutters'
Honeycombed workings.
Now his stained face
Reposes at Aarhus.

II

I could risk blasphemy,
Consecrate the cauldron bog
Our holy ground and pray
Him to make germinate

The scattered, ambushed
Flesh of labourers,
Stockinged corpses
Laid out in the farmyards,

Tell-tale skin and teeth
Flecking the sleepers
Of four young brothers, trailed
For miles along the lines.

III
Something of his freedom
As he rode the tumbril
Should come to me, driving,
Saying the names

Tollund, Grabaulle, Nebelgard,
Watching the pointing hands
Of country people,
Not knowing their tongue.

Out there in Jutland
In the old man-killing parishes
I will feel lost,
Unhappy and at home.

SUMMER HOME
I
Was it wind off the dumps
or something in heat

dogging us, the summer gone sour,
a fouled nest incubating somewhere?

Whose fault, I wondered, inquisitor
of the possessed air.

To realize suddenly,
whip off the mat

that was larval, moving —
and scald, scald, scald.

II
Bushing the door, my arms full
of wild cherry and rhododendron,
I hear her small lost weeping
through the hall, that bells and hoarsens
on my name, my name.

O love, here is the blame.

The loosened flowers between us
gather in, compose
for a May altar of sorts.
These frank and falling blooms
soon taint to a sweet chrism.

Attend. Anoint the wound.

III
O we tented our wound all right
under the homely sheet

and lay as if the cold flat of a blade
had winded us.

More and more I postulate
thick healings, like now

as you bend in the shower
water lives down the tilting stoups of your breasts.

IV
With a final
unmusical drive
long grains begin
to open and split

ahead and once more
we sap
the white, trodden
path to the heart.

V
My children weep out the hot foreign night.
We walk the floor, my foul mouth takes it out
On you and we lie stiff till dawn
Attends the pillow, and the maize, and vine

That holds its filling burden to the light.
Yesterday rocks sang when we tapped
Stalactites in the cave's old, dripping dark —
Our love calls tiny as a tuning fork.

VIKING DUBLIN: TRIAL PIECES

I
It could be a jaw-bone
or a rib or a portion cut
from something sturdier:
anyhow, a small outline

was incised, a cage
or trellis to conjure in.
Like a child's tongue
following the toils

of his calligraphy,
like an eel swallowed
in a basket of eels,
the line amazes itself

eluding the hand
that fed it,
a bill in flight,
a swimming nostril.

II
These are trial pieces,
the craft's mystery
improvised on bone:
foliage, bestiaries,

interlacings elaborate
as the netted routes
of ancestry and trade.
That have to be

magnified on display
so that the nostril
is a migrant prow
sniffing the Liffey,

swanning it up to the ford,
dissembling itself
in antler combs, bone pins,
coins, weights, scale-pans.

III
Like a long sword
sheathed in its moisting
burial clays,
the keel stuck fast

in the slip of the bank,
its clinker-built hull
spined and plosive
as *Dublin.*

And now we reach in
for shards of the vertebrae,
the ribs of hurdle,
the mother-wet caches —

and for this trial piece
incised by a child,
a longship, a buoyant
migrant line.

IV
That enters my longhand,
turns cursive, unscarfing
a zoomorphic wake,
a worm of thought

I follow into the mud.
I am Hamlet the Dane,
skull-handler, parablist,
smeller of rot

in the state, infused
with its poisons,
pinioned by ghosts
and affections,

murders and pieties,
coming to consciousness
by jumping in graves,
dithering, blathering.

V
Come fly with me,
come sniff the wind
with the expertise
of the Vikings—

neighbourly, scoretaking
killers, haggers
and hagglers, gombeen-men,
hoarders of grudges and gain.

With a butcher's aplomb
they spread out your lungs
and made you warm wings
for your shoulders.

Old fathers, be with us.
Old cunning assessors
of feuds and of sites
for ambush or town.

VI
'Did you ever hear tell,'
said Jimmy Farrell,
'of the skulls they have
in the city of Dublin?

White skulls and black skulls
and yellow skulls, and some
with full teeth, and some
haven't only but one,'

and compounded history
in the pan of 'an old Dane,
maybe, was drowned
in the Flood.'

My words lick around
cobbled quays, go hunting
lightly as pampooties
over the skull-capped ground.

KINSHIP

I

Kinned by hieroglyphic
peat on a spreadfield
to the strangled victim,
the love-nest in the bracken,

I step through origins
like a dog turning
its memories of wilderness
on the kitchen mat:

the bog floor shakes,
water cheeps and lisps
as I walk down
rushes and heather.

I love this turf-face,
its black incisions,
the cooped secrets
of process and ritual;

I love the spring
off the ground,
each bank a gallows drop,
each open pool

the unstopped mouth
of an urn, a moon-drinker,
not to be sounded
by the naked eye.

II

Quagmire, swampland, morass:
the slime kingdoms,
domains of the cold-blooded,
of mud pads and dirtied eggs.

But *bog*
meaning soft,
the fall of windless rain,
pupil of amber.

Ruminant ground,
digestion of mollusc

and seed-pod,
deep pollen bin.

Earth-pantry, bone-vault,
sun-bank, enbalmer
of votive goods
and sabred fugitives.

Insatiable bride.
Sword-swallower,
casket, midden,
floe of history.

Ground that will strip
its dark side,
nesting ground,
outback of my mind.

III
I found a turf-spade
hidden under bracken,
laid flat, and overgrown
with a green fog.

As I raised it
the soft lips of the growth
muttered and split,
a tawny rut

opening at my feet
like a shed skin,
the shaft wettish
as I sank it upright

and beginning to
steam in the sun.
And now they have twinned
that obelisk:

among the stones,
under a bearded cairn
a love-nest is disturbed,
catkin and bog-cotton tremble

as they raise up
the cloven oak-limb.
I stand at the edge of centuries
facing a goddess.

IV
This centre holds
and spreads,
sump and seedbed,
a bag of waters

and a melting grave.
The mothers of autumn
sour and sink,
ferments of husk and leaf

deepen their ochres.
Mosses come to a head,
heather unseeds,
brackens deposit

their bronze.
This is the vowel of earth
dreaming its root
in flowers and snow,

mutation of weathers
and seasons,
a windfall composing
the floor it rots into.

I grew out of all this
like a weeping willow
inclined to
the appetites of gravity.

V
The hand carved felloes
of the turf-cart wheels
buried in a litter
of turf mould,

the cupid's bow
of the tail-board,

the socketed lips
of the cribs:

I deified the man
who rode there,
god of the waggon,
the hearth-feeder.

I was his privileged
attendant, a bearer
of bread and drink,
the squire of his circuits.

When summer died
and wives forsook the fields
we were abroad,
saluted, given right-of-way.

Watch our progress
down the haw-lit hedges,
my manly pride
when he speaks to me.

VI
And you, Tacitus,
observe how I make my grove
on an old crannog
piled by the fearful dead:

a desolate peace.
Our mother ground
is sour with the blood
of her faithful,

they lie gargling
in her sacred heart
as the legions stare
from the ramparts.

Come back to this
'island of the ocean'
where nothing will suffice.
Read the inhumed faces

of casualty and victim;
report us fairly,
how we slaughter
for the common good

and shave the heads
of the notorious,
how the goddess swallows
our love and terror.

A CONSTABLE CALLS

His bicycle stood at the window-sill,
The rubber cowl of a mud-splasher
Skirting the front mudguard,
Its fat black handlegrips

Heating in sunlight, the 'spud'
Of the dynamo gleaming and cocked back,
The pedal treads hanging relieved
Of the boot of the law.

His cap was upside down
On the floor, next his chair.
The line of its pressure ran like a bevel
In his slightly sweating hair.

He had unstrapped
The heavy ledger, and my father
Was making tillage returns
In acres, roods, and perches.

Arithmetic and fear.
I sat staring at the polished holster
With its buttoned flap, the braid cord
Looped into the revolver butt.

'Any other root crops?
Mangolds? Marrowstems? Anything like that?'
'No.' But was there not a line
Of turnips where the seed ran out

In the potato field? I assumed
Small guilts and sat
Imagining the black hole in the barracks.
He stood up, shifted the baton-case

Further round on his belt,
Closed the domesday book,
Fitted his cap back with two hands,
And looked at me as he said goodbye.

A shadow bobbed in the window.
He was snapping the carrier spring
Over the ledger. His boot pushed off
And the bicycle ticked, ticked, ticked.

EXPOSURE

It is December in Wicklow:
Alders dripping, birches
Inheriting the last light,
The ash tree cold to look at.

A comet that was lost
Should be visible at sunset,
Those million tons of light
Like a glimmer of haws and rose-hips,

And I sometimes see a falling star.
If I could come on meteorite!
Instead I walk through damp leaves,
Husks, the spent flukes of autumn,

Imagining a hero
On some muddy compound,
His gift like a slingstone
Whirled for the desperate.

How did I end up like this?
I often think of my friends'
Beautiful prismatic counselling
And the anvil brains of some who hate me

As I sit weighing and weighing
My responsible *tristia*.
For what? For the ear? For the people?
For what is said behind-backs?

Rain comes down through the alders,
Its low conducive voices
Mutter about let-downs and erosions
And yet each drop recalls

The diamond absolutes.
I am neither internee nor informer;
An inner émigré, grown long-haired
And thoughtful; a wood-kerne

Escaped from the massacre,
Taking protective colouring
From bole and bark, feeling
Every wind that blows,

Who, blowing up these sparks
For their meagre heat, have missed
The once-in-a-lifetime portent,
The comet's pulsing rose.

CASUALTY

He would drink by himself
And raise a weathered thumb
Towards the high shelf,
Calling another rum
And blackcurrant, without
Having to raise his voice,
Or order a quick stout
By a lifting of the eyes
And a discreet dumb-show
Or pulling off the top;
At closing time would go
In waders and peaked cap
Out into the dark,
A dole-kept breadwinner
But a natural for work.

I loved his whole manner,
Sure-footed but too sly,
His deadpan sidling tact,
His fisherman's quick eye
And turned observant back.

Incomprehensible
To him, my other life.
Sometimes, on his high stool,
Too busy with his knife
At a tobacco plug
And not meeting my eye,
In the pause after a slug
He mentioned poetry.
We would be on our own
And, always politic
And shy of condescension,
I would manage by some trick
To switch the talk to eels
Or lore of the horse and cart
Or the Provisionals.

But my kept wilting art
His turned back watches too:
He was blown to wet bits
Out drinking in a curfew
That wiser citizens
Observed behind closed doors
When we mourned the thirteen killed
By British paratroopers.

It was a day of cold
Raw silence, wind-blown
Surplice and soutane:
Rained-on, flower-laden
Coffin after coffin
Seemed to float from the door
Of the packed cathedral
Like blossoms on slow water.
The common funeral
Unrolled its swaddling band,
Lapping, tightening
Till we were braced and bound
Like brothers in a ring.

But he would not be held
At home by his own crowd
Whatever threats were phoned,
Whatever black flags waved.
I see him as he turned
In that bombed offending place,
Remorse fused with terror
In his still knowable face,
His cornered outfaced stare
Blinding in the flash.

He had gone miles away
For he drank like a fish
Nightly, naturally
Swimming towards the lure
Of warm lit-up places,
The blurred mesh and murmur
Drifting among glasses
In the gregarious smoke.
How culpable was he
That last night when he broke
Our tribe's complicity?
"Now you're supposed to be
An educated man,"
I hear him say. "Puzzle me
The right answer to that one."

I missed his funeral,
Those quiet walkers
And sideways talkers
Shoaling out of his lane
To the respectable
Purring of the hearse...
They move in equal pace
With the habitual
Slow consolation
Of a dawdling engine,
The line lifted, hand
Over fist, cold sunshine
On the water, the land
Banked under fog: that morning
I was taken in his boat,
The screw purling, turning
Indolent fathoms white,

I tasted freedom with him.
To get out early, haul
Steadily off the bottom,
Dispraise the catch, and smile
As you find a rhythm
Working you, slow mile by mile,
Into your proper haunt
Somewhere, well out, beyond...

Dawn sniffing revenant,
Plodder through midnight rain,
Question me again.

A POSTCARD FROM NORTH ANTRIM
In memory of Sean Armstrong

A lone figure is waving
From the thin line of a bridge
Of ropes and slats, slung
Dangerously out between
The cliff-top and the pillar rock.
A nineteenth century wind.
Dulse-pickers. Sea campions.

A postcard for you, Sean,
And that's you, swinging alone,
Antic, half-afraid,
In your gallowglass's beard
And swallow-tail of serge:
The Carrick-a-Rede Rope Bridge
Ghost-written on sepia.

Or should it be your houseboat
Ethnically furnished,
Redolent of grass?
Should we discover you
Beside those warm-planked, democratic wharves
Among the twilights and guitars
Of Sausalito?

Drop-out on a come-back,
Prince of no-man's land
With your head in clouds or sand,

You were the clown
Social worker of the town
Until your candid forehead stopped
A pointblank teatime bullet.

Get up from your blood on the floor.
Here's another boat
In grass by the lough shore,
Turf smoke, a wired hen-run —
Your local, hoped for, unfound commune.
Now recite me *William Bloat,*
Sing of *the Calabar*

Or of Henry Joy McCracken
Who kissed his Mary Ann
On the gallows at Cornmarket.
Or Ballycastle Fair.
"Give us the raw bar!"
"Sing it by brute force
If you forget the air."

Yet something in your voice
Stayed nearly shut.
Your voice was a harrassed pulpit
Leading the melody
It kept at bay,
It was independent, rattling, non-transcendent
Ulster — old decency

And Old Bushmills,
Soda farls, strong tea,
New rope, rock salt, kale plants,
Potato-bread and Woodbine.
Wind through the concrete vents
Of a border check-point.
Cold zinc nailed for a peace line.

Fifteen years ago, come this October,
Crowded on your floor,
I got my arm round Marie's shoulder
For the first time.
"Oh, Sir Jasper, do not touch me!"
You roared across at me,
Chorus-leading, splashing out the wine.

GLANMORE SONNETS

III

This evening the cuckoo and the corncrake
(So much, too much) consorted at twilight.
It was all crepuscular and iambic.
Out on the field a baby rabbit
Took his bearings, and I knew the deer
(I've seen them too from the window of the house,
Like connoisseurs, inquisitive of air)
Were careful under larch and May-green spruce.
I had said earlier, "I won't relapse
From this strange loneliness I've brought us to.
Dorothy and William —" She interrupts:
"You're not going to compare us two...?"
Outside a rustling and twig-combing breeze
Refreshes and relents. Is cadences.

VII

Thunderlight on the split logs: big raindrops
At body heat and lush with omen
Spattering dark on the hatchet iron.
This morning when a magpie with jerky steps
Inspected a horse asleep beside the wood
I thought of dew on armour and carrion.
What would I meet, blood-boltered, on the road?
How deep into the woodpile sat the toad?
What welters through this dark hush on the crops?
Do you remember that pension in Les Landes
Where the old one rocked and rocked and rocked
A mongol in her lap, to little songs?
Come to me quick, I am upstairs shaking.
My all of you birchwood in lightning.

THE OTTER

When you plunged
The light of Tuscany wavered
And swung through the pool
From top to bottom.

I loved your wet head and smashing crawl,
Your fine swimmer's back and shoulders
Surfacing and surfacing again
This year and every year since.

I sat dry-throated on the warm stones.
You were beyond me.
The mellowed clarities, the grape-deep air
Thinned and disappointed.

Thank God for the slow loadening.
When I hold you now
We are close and deep
As the atmosphere on water.

My two hands are plumbed water.
You are my palpable, lithe
Otter of memory
In the pool of the moment,

Turning to swim on your back,
Each silent, thigh-shaking kick
Re-tilting the light,
Heaving the cool at your neck.

And suddenly you're out,
Back again, intent as ever,
Heavy and frisky in your freshened pelt,
Printing the stones.

SONG

A rowan like a lipsticked girl.
Between the bye-road and the main road
Alder trees at a wet and dripping distance
Stand off among the rushes.

There are the mud-flowers of dialect
And the immortelles of perfect pitch
And that moment when the bird sings very close
To the music of what happens.

SELECT BIBLIOGRAPHY
OF TWENTIETH CENTURY IRISH POETRY

W. B. Yeats (1865-1939)
  Collected Poems (1952)
AE (George Russell) (1867-1936)
  Collected Poems (1935)
J. M. Synge (1871-1909)
  Collected Works: Poems (1962)
Thomas MacDonagh (1878-1916)
  Poetical Works (1916)
  Poems (1920)
Oliver St. John Gogarty (1878-1957)
  Collected Poems (1951)
Seumas O'Sullivan (1879-1958)
  Collected Poems (1940)
Joseph Campbell (1879-1944)
  Poems, ed. Austin Clarke (1963)
Padraic Colum (1881-1972)
  Collected Poems (1953)
James Joyce (1882-1941)
  Collected Poems (1936)
James Stephens (1882-1950)
  Collected Poems (1954)
Joseph Plunkett (1887-1916)
  The Circle and the Sword (1911)
  Poems (1916)
Francis Ledgewidge (1891-1917)
  Complete Poems (1974)
Thomas MacGreevy (1894-1967)
  Collected Poems (1971)
F. R. Higgins (1896-1941)
  Island Blood (1925)
  The Dark Breed (1927)
  The Gap of Brightness (1940)
Austin Clarke (1896-1974)
  Collected Poems (1974)

Monk Gibbon (1896-   )
  Collected Poems (1951)
  The Velvet Bow (1972)
Patrick MacDonagh (1902-1961)
  A Leaf in the Wind (1929)
  Shamrock Leaves (1936)
  The Vestal Fire: a poem (1941)
John Lyle Donaghy (1902-1947)
  Selected Poems (1939)
Ewart Milne (1903-   )
  Diamond Cut Diamond.
  Selected Poems (1950)
  Life Aboreal (1953)
  Galion: a poem (1953)
  A Garland for the Green (1962)
  Time Stopped (1967)
  Drift of Pinions (1976)
  Cantata under Orion (1976)
Patrick Kavanagh (1905-1967)
  Collected Poems (1964)
Brian Coffey (1905-   )
  Third Person (1938)
  Dice Thrown Never Will Annul
  Chance (1965)
  Monster (1966)
  The Time, The Place (1969)
  Selected Poems (1971)
  Irish University Review, Vol.5,
  No.1, (1975)
  The Big Laugh (1976)
Padraic Fallon (1905-1974)
  Poems (1974)
Samuel Beckett (1906-   )
  Collected Poems in English and
  French (1977)

Louis MacNeice (1907-1963)
  Collected Poems (1966)
John Hewitt (1907-   )
  Collected Poems 1932-1967 (1968)
  Out of My Time: Poems 1967-74
    (1974)
  Time Enough (1976)
  The Rain Dance (1978)
Denis Devlin (1908-1959)
  Collected Poems (1964)
  Selected Poems (1964)
Robert Farren (1909-   )
  Selected Poems (1951)
W. R. Rodgers (1909-1969)
  Collected Poems (1971)
Sean Jennett (1910-   )
  Always Adam (1943)
  The Cloth of Flesh (1945)
  The Sun and Old Stones (1961)
  Deserts of England (1964)
Donagh MacDonagh (1912-1968)
  The Hungry Grass (1947)
  A Warning to Conquerors (1968)
Valentin Iremonger (1918-   )
  Reservations (1945)
  Horan's Field and Other
    Reservations (1972)
Eoghan O Tuairisc (1919-   )
  Lux Aeterna (1964)
  The Weekend of Dermot and
    Grace (1964)
  New Passages (1973)
Robert Greacen (1920-   )
  Poems from Ulster (1942)
  One Recent Evening (1944)
  The Undying Day (1948)
  A Garland for Captain Fox (1975)
Kevin Faller (1920-   )
  Lyric and Script (1947)

Genesis (1953)
Island Lyrics (1963)
Lament for the Bull Island (1973)
Roy McFadden (1922-   )
  Swords and Ploughshares (1943)
  Flowers for a Lady (1945)
  The Heart's Townland (1947)
  Elegy for the Dead of the
    Princess Victoria (1953)
  Versifications (1977)
Eithne Strong (1923-   )
  Songs of Living (1961)
  Sarah, In Passing (1974)
Padraic Fiacc (1924-   )
  By the Black Stream (1969)
  Odour of Blood (1973)
  Nights in the Bad Place (1977)
Alfred Allen (1925-   )
  Clashenure Skyline (1971)
  Interrogations (1975)
Jerome Kiely (1925-   )
  The Griffon Sings (1966)
Anthony Cronin (1925-   )
  Poems (1958)
  R.M.S. Titanic (1973)
  Collected Poems (1973)
Francis Harvey (1925-   )
  In the Light of the Stones (1978)
Richard Murphy (1927-   )
  The Archaeology of Love (1955)
  Sailing to an Island (1965)
  The Battle of Aughrim (1968)
  High Island (1974)
Richard Kell (1927-   )
  Control Tower (1962)
Pearse Hutchinson (1927-   )
  Tongue Without Hands (1963)
  Faoistin Bhacach (1968)
  Expansions (1969)

Watching the Morning Grow (1972)
The Frost is All Over (1975)
Basil Payne (1928-   )
   Sunlight on a Square (1961)
   Love in the Afternoon (1971)
   Another Kind of Optimism (1974)
Thomas Kinsella (1928-   )
   Another September (1958)
   Downstream (1962)
   Nightwalker (1968)
   The Táin (1969)
   A Selected Life (1972)
   Selected Poems (1973)
   New Poems (1973)
   The Good Fight (1973)
   Vertical Man (1973)
   One (1974)
   A Technical Supplement (1976)
   Song of the Night (1978)
   The Messenger (1978)
Patrick Galvin (1929-   )
   Irish Songs of Resistance (1955)
   Heart of Grace (1957)
   Christ in London (1960)
   The Wood Burners (1970)
John Montague (1929-   )
   Forms of Exile (1958)
   Poisoned Lands (1961, 1977)
   A Chosen Light (1967)
   Tides (1970, 1978)
   The Rough Field (1972)
   A Slow Dance (1975)
   The Great Cloak (1978)
John Jordan (1930-   )
   Patrician Stations (1971)
   A Raft from Flotsam (1975)
   Blood and Stations (1976)
Richard Weber (1932-   )
   Lady and Gentleman (1963)

Stephen's Green Revisited (1968)
   A Few Small Ones (1971)
James Simmons (1933-   )
   Late but in Earnest (1967)
   In the Wilderness (1969)
   Energy to Burn (1971)
   *The Long Summer Still to
   Come* (1973)
   West Strand Visions (1974)
   Judy Garland and the Cold War (1976)
   Selected Poems ed. Edna Longley (1978)
James Liddy (1934-   )
   Esau My Kingdom for a Drink (1962)
   In a Blue Smoke (1964)
   Blue Mountain (1968)
   *A Munster Song of Love and
   War* (1971)
   Beaudelaire's Barroom Flowers (1976)
   Corca Bascinn (1977)
Desmond O'Grady (1935-   )
   Chords and Orchestrations (1956)
   Reilly (1961)
   The Dark Edge of Europe (1967)
   The Dying Gaul (1968)
   Hellas (1971)
   Separations (1973)
   The Gododdin (1977)
   Sing Me Creation (1977)
   A Limerick Rake (1978)
   The Headgear of a Tribe,
   new and selected poems (1978)
James McAuley (1935-   )
   Observations (1960)
   A New Address (1965)
   After the Blizzard (1975)
Brendan Kennelly (1936-   )
   Selected Poems (1971)
   Bread (1971)
   Love Cry (1972)

Salvation, the Stranger (1972)
The Voices (1973)
Shelley in Dublin (1974)
A Kind of Trust (1975)
New and Selected Poems (1976)
Islandman (1977)
Desmond Egan (1936-   )
   Midland (1973)
   Leaves (1975)
   Siege (1976)
   Woodcutter (1978)
Sydney Bernard Smith (1936-   )
   Girl with Violin (1968)
Conleth Ellis (1937-   )
   Poems (1961)
   This Ripening Time (1966)
   Under the Stone (1971)
   Fomhar na nGéanna (1975)
George McWhirter (1939-   )
   Catalan Poems (1971)
   Queen of the Sea (1976)
   Twenty-Five (1978)
Seamus Heaney (1939-   )
   Death of a Naturalist (1966)
   Door into the Dark (1969)
   Wintering Out (1972)
   North (1975)
Michael Longley (1939-   )
   An Exploded View (1968)
   No Continuing City (1969)
   Lares (1972)
   Man Lying on a Wall (1976)
Seamus Deane (1940-   )
   Gradual Wars (1972)
   Rumours (1977)
Michael Hartnett (1941-   )
   Selected Poems (1970)
   Gipsy Ballads (1973)
   A Farewell to English (1975,1978)

The Retreat of Ita Cagney /
Cúlú Ide (1975)
Poems in English (1977)
Prisoners (1977)
Adharca Broic (1978)

Sean Clarkin (1941-   )
   Without Frenzy (1974)
Derek Mahon (1941-   )
   Night Crossing (1968)
   Beyond Howth Head (1970)
   Lives (1972)
   The Snow Party (1975)
Eilean Ní Chuilleanain (1942-   )
   Acts and Monuments (1972)
   Odysseus Meets the Ghosts of
   the Women (1973)
   Site of Ambush (1975)
   The Second Voyage (1978)
Michael Smith (1942-   )
   With the Woodnymphs (1968)
   Dedications (1968)
   Times and Locations (1972)
   Pilgrimage (1976)
Geoffrey Squires (1942-   )
   Drowned Stones (1976)
Macdara Woods (1942-   )
   Early Morning Matins (1972)
   Decimal D. Sec. Drinks in a
   Bar in Marakesch (1970)
Augustus Young (1943-   )
   On Loaning Hill (1972)
   Rosemaries (1976)
John F. Deane (1943-   )
   Stalking After Time (1977)
Paul Durcan (1944-   )
   O Westport in the Light of
   Asia Minor (1975)
   Teresa's Bar (1976)

John Ennis (1944-   )
   Night on Hibernia (1976)
   Dolmen Hill (1978)
Michael Brophy (1945-   )
   A Tired Tribe (1976)
Eavan Boland (1945-   )
   New Territory (1967)
   The War Horse (1975)
Brian Lynch (1945-   )
   Endsville (with Paul Durcan)
      (1967)
   No Die Cast (1969)
   Outside the Pheasantry (1976)
Tom Mathews (1945-   )
   Interior Din (1969)
   Full Stop (1973)
Daniel Reardon (1946-   )
   In the Lion House (1974)
Michael Foley (1947-   )
   Heil Hitler (1969)
   The Acne and the Ecstasy (1973)
   Through the Gateless Gate (1976)
Paul Murray (1947-   )
   Ritual Poems (1971)

Trevor Joyce (1947-   )
   Sole Glum Trek (1967)
   Watches (1969)
   Pentahedron (1971)
   The Poems of Sweeney Peregrine
      (1976)
Hugh Maxton (1947-   )
   Stones (1970)
   The Noise of the Fields (1976)
Frank Ormsby (1947-   )
   Ripe for Company (1971)
   Business as Usual (1973)
   A Store of Candles (1977)

Ciaran Carson (1948-   )
   The Insular Celts (1973)
   The New Estate (1976)
Richard Ryan (1949-   )
   Ledges (1970)
   Ravenswood (1973)
Peter Fallon (1951-   )
   Among the Walls (1971)
   Coincidence of Flesh (1972)
   The First Affair (1974)
   A Gentler Birth (1976)
   Victims (1977)
   The Speaking Stones (1978)
Paul Muldoon (1951-   )
   Knowing My Place (1971)
   New Weather (1973)
   Mules (1977)
Gerard Smyth (1951-   )
   The Flags are Quiet (1969)
   Twenty Poems (1970)
   Orchestra of Silence (1971)
   World Without End (1977)
Harry Clifton (1952-   )
   The Walls of Carthage (1977)
Gerald Dawe (1952-   )
   Heritages (1976)
   Blood and Moon (1976)
   Sheltering Places (1978)
Thomas McCarthy (1954-   )
   The First Convention (1978)
Aidan Carl Mathews (1956-   )
   Windfalls (1977)